'Like so many of the best books, *Change Sta[...]* personal application. The forty questions i[...] groups on a deep, useful, reflective journey th[...] living person should be interested in.'

Jim Knight *Founder and CEO of Instructional Coaching Group.*

'*Change Starts Here* is a beautifully crafted roadmap, guiding readers through the often tangled forest of organisational change. Shane Leaning and Efraim Lerner act as expert trail guides, providing both a compass and a lantern to navigate the complexities of transformation in education.

The authors don't just hand you a map and wish you luck; instead, they walk alongside you, encouraging you to pause at critical junctures to reflect on the terrain. Their "double diamond" framework feels like a sturdy bridge over turbulent waters, connecting the islands of aspiration and reality. Each stage of the journey – Connect, Discover, Define and Align, etc., is mapped with powerful questions which feel like trail markers, ensuring you never lose your way.

This book is not a pre-packaged tour; it's a call to adventure, inviting everyone in the community: teachers, leaders, parents and even students, to join the expedition. The stories sprinkled throughout serve as both cautionary tales and inspiring beacons, reminding us that while the forest may be dense, the view from the summit is worth every step.

Leaning and Lerner's focus on dialogue and inclusivity transforms change from a lonely climb into a shared hike, where every voice adds strength to the collective effort. Their emphasis on psychological safety and shared values as the foundation for meaningful change ensures that the path is not only clear but sustainable for future travellers.

For anyone ready to embark on the challenging yet rewarding journey of educational transformation, *Change Starts Here* is more than a book – it's the guide, the gear and the spirit you need to reach the summit together.'

Dr Haili Hughes *Director of Education at IRIS Connect and Principal Lecturer in Professional Development at the University of Sunderland*

'Many of us working in schools will recognise the 'change fatigue' that comes from the constant cycle of new initiatives, which do not always yield the improvements we seek. We also know that the problems we face in schools are complex, and cannot be addressed by simple, one-size-fits-all solutions.

In *Change Starts Here*, Shane Leaning and Efraim Lerner make the compelling case that our tendency to look outward for answers is leading to a loss of organisational confidence. By outsourcing thinking, we miss opportunities to build deep contextual expertise and empower the professionals doing the work on the ground in our schools. Meaningful change, they argue, must come from within, deeply anchored in the school community, responsive to its unique challenges and respecting its strengths.

Drawing on their extensive international experience of school improvement and leadership development, the authors offer a practical, easily applicable framework to guide the deep thinking needed to build meaningful change. They do not shy away from its complexities but embrace it as a dynamic process and a collective endeavour. They show how, by starting with asking powerful questions, we can engage everyone in our school communities in open, honest reflection and deep purposeful collaboration, building and shaping solutions together. This is how we break the cycle of change without improvement and reclaim our profession.

Change Starts Here is a salve for a broken system. It is a call to stop waiting for someone else to take action, but to be the change we seek: a manifesto for *people-powered* change which empowers and humanises. It is a deeply important read for everyone who works in education.'

Sam Gibbs *Director of Education, Greater Manchester Education Trust, UK*

Change Starts Here

In education, change is inevitable. But despite this, most school change projects falter because they miss what matters most: the human element. *Change Starts Here* revolutionises how we think about educational change by putting people back at the heart of the process.

This groundbreaking book unveils a practical approach that transforms how schools navigate change. At its core lies the innovative double diamond model, a powerful framework that helps school communities discover what truly matters to them and co-create solutions that stick. Through 40 carefully crafted questions and real-world case studies from schools across the world, the authors demonstrate how to replace rigid, top-down directives with authentic, community-driven change.

Whether you're wrestling with curriculum reform, teaching development, or new technology, *Change Starts Here* will help you build consensus, honour diverse perspectives, and create lasting impact. Essential reading for school leaders, teachers, and anyone passionate about making meaningful change in education.

Shane Leaning is an organisational coach and supports international schools globally. He hosts the chart-topping school leadership podcast, Education Leaders, and is co-founder of Work Collaborative.

Efraim Lerner is founder of Brıne and co-founder of Work Collaborative. He works globally with organisations to drive innovation and sustainable change and serves on EdTech advisory boards and professional development platforms.

Change Starts Here

What if Everything Your School
Needed Was Right in Front of You?

Shane Leaning and Efraim Lerner

Routledge
Taylor & Francis Group

LONDON AND NEW YORK

Designed cover image: Shane Leaning and Efraim Lerner

First published 2026
by Routledge
4 Park Square, Milton Park, Abingdon, Oxon OX14 4RN

and by Routledge
605 Third Avenue, New York, NY 10158

Routledge is an imprint of the Taylor & Francis Group, an informa business

© 2026 Shane Leaning and Efraim Lerner

British Library Cataloguing-in-Publication Data
A catalogue record for this book is available from the British Library

ISBN: 978-1-032-97925-0 (hbk)
ISBN: 978-1-032-97924-3 (pbk)
ISBN: 978-1-003-59614-1 (ebk)

DOI: 10.4324/9781003596141

Typeset in Celeste and Optima
by Apex CoVantage, LLC

Printed and bound in Great Britain by Bell & Bain Ltd, Glasgow

NP105842
For Product Safety Concerns and Information please contact our EU representative Taylor & Francis Verlag GmbH, Kaufingerstraße 24, 80331 München, Germany GPSR@taylorandfrancis.com

This book is dedicated to Emma and Shterna Sarah; your unwavering support and love make us better versions of ourselves. This book is a testament to the power of true collaboration and the profound impact that we can have when we see the innate value in each other. Thank you for inspiring us every day.

Contents

Contents

List of 40 Questions

List of 40 Questions

Foreword

It is a sad truth that the education system is full of change that has failed. The same is true in health, in other areas of public service and throughout the private sector and business. When I talk about failed change, I mean where the change has not improved things as much as planned, where there has been no improvement at all or where (and I include change projects I have led here) where things have actually got worse.

There are many reasons why change does not always bring the improvement we hope for or intend. Viviane Robinson argued in 2017[1] that too often we assume that change will lead to improvement and she suggests that leaders should assume the opposite and think more carefully about creating the conditions for change to succeed. Sixty years before Robinson was writing this about education, the American industrialist W Edwards Deming was inspiring the post-war Japanese economic miracle with his 14 Points – an approach to change an innovation underpinned by a robust and clear framework.

In The Education Alliance, a multi-academy trust of 12 schools in Yorkshire that I have the enormous privilege of leading, we obsess about delivering improvement through change that is well planned, effectively implemented and invite great people from all areas of our organisation to become part of the process. We know that positive change never happens by accident; it happens through robust processes and brilliant people. Both Robinson and Deming influence our thinking strongly. With this book, Shane Leaning and Efraim Lerner join that short list.

This is a book about change. It is a book that recognises that change can be exciting, scary or painful and that often it is all those things, all at once. It is a book that reflects the complexity of leading change and one that talks honestly and compellingly about a crisis in confidence in leadership in schools as so many leaders drown under competing pressures and binary arguments about education and schools.

But it is also a book that shines with hope. This is not hope based on groundless optimism but hope rooted deeply in one of the most interesting, practical and innovative solutions to change in education I have seen. The authors offer a roadmap or framework for change. They have taken the British Design Council's double diamond model and adapted it thoughtfully and intelligently, not just to make it applicable to education, but because humans are beautifully messy and it is only by embracing the 'beautiful complexity of human interaction' that deep, lasting, positive change can come.

And in the end, this is a book about people, written by two people who truly believe in others. Time and again they make the point powerfully that change comes not just through leaders or people with particular job titles, but through all of us. They clearly state that 'each person has a genuine value, regardless of position' and that belief runs through every page of the book. It comes to life through the stories they tell and ultimately it is power and potential of people that their adapted double diamond model seeks to unlock.

This is a wonderful book, the 'deeply personal' work of two wonderful people.

Jonny Uttley
December 2024

Note

1   Robinson, V. M. J. (2017). *Reduce Change to Increase Improvement.* Corwin.

Acknowledgements

This book is a testament to collaboration. Despite living on opposite ends of the world and having met only to present the work that would become this book, we've discovered that distance is no barrier when surrounded by the right community. The 'village' that has supported us – friends, family, and fellow educators – has made these ideas not just possible, but real.

While it's impossible to acknowledge everyone who has contributed to this journey, we must express our profound gratitude to those who have shaped our thinking and supported our work. Jim Knight, Jonny Uttley, Sam Gibbs, James Harding, Jonathan Boymal, and Dr Haili Hughes, to name but a few, provided invaluable feedback that helped refine and strengthen our ideas.

A serendipitous meeting with Ola Handford in a Shanghai coffee shop introduced us to the British Design Council's double diamond model, which became foundational to our work. Catherine Cooke's subsequent feedback on our adaptation of this model proved invaluable. Of course we are deeply thankful to the British Design Council for their work.

We are deeply indebted to Annamarie from Routledge for her trust, guidance, and unwavering support. Our thanks also go to Sam Gibbs and Brad Busch for connecting us with Routledge, and to the reviewers whose thoughtful feedback transformed our good ideas into great ones.

Neil Mullen deserves special recognition for creating the space that allowed us both to do our best thinking. The coaching fraternity in education, particularly Iain Henderson and Jim Knight, has been instrumental in inspiring our approach and supporting the development of these ideas.

To all the researchers, practitioners, thought leaders, and community whose work has paved the way for ours, know that your contributions, both seen and unseen, have helped shape these pages.

What began as a simple vision has grown into something far greater than ourselves, and for that, we are profoundly grateful.

A Word from Shane

Every great journey has its foundations, and mine begins with my parents and brothers. Their unfaltering belief in me has been a constant source of strength, showing me what true support looks like. And Emma, thank you for supporting me through everything. This book could not be here if it were not for your patience, love, and support.

I've been fortunate to learn from exceptional leaders like Stacy Wallace and Chris Wathern, who shaped my understanding of what leadership can be. And to Wendy Letherland, who first inspired me to become a teacher, your influence continues to guide my work. Each of you has helped create ripples that extend through all my work. Of course I must also mention the wonderful podcast community around my show, *Education Leaders*. Whether you have been a guest or a listener, your connection and ideas have shaped me.

A Word from Efraim

My journey begins with my parents. To my mother, whose passion for education and thoughtful approach to life shaped my earliest understanding of its power, thank you for being my first and greatest teacher.

Acknowledgements

And to Abba, your selfless devotion to others taught me what it means to lead with love and integrity, lessons that guide me every day as a parent. To my brother Eli, your steady presence and unwavering support have been a constant source of strength, especially in challenging moments. To Rod, your faith in me gave me the courage to take the next step; your encouragement has meant more than you know.

Growing up, my surname often drew comments about education, but it became a badge of pride, shaped by role models like my Uncle Phil and Aunt Bernice, of blessed memory, whose dedication to learning and community continue to inspire me. To the extended Moses family, thank you for embracing me as one of your own with such warmth and generosity. A special mention to Tata Esther; your open heart and welcoming home created a nurturing space for my ideas to take root. To my lifelong friends, in Australia and across the globe, thank you for reminding me that true connection transcends distance. Your kindness and support have been a source of strength and encouragement throughout this journey. To my teachers, colleagues, and students, your impact is woven into every word of this work. Rabbi Shaul Rosenblatt and the RTA team, thank you for showing me the profound potential in every moment and the depth of connection beyond words.

To G-d, the source of all inspiration, thank you for the privilege of exploring and sharing the beauty of this world. Finally, to my beloved wife, Shterna Sarah, and our daughters, Hadassa and Anaelle, your love, strength, and belief in me are my greatest blessings. Each of you have contributed to this work in ways that extend far beyond these pages.

Introduction

Heraclitus said it best:

> The only constant in life is change.

Nothing stands still; only change persists. This phrase is purposely paradoxical, but it underscores the reality that change is always happening, whether we are prepared for it or not. And nowhere is this truer than in education.

Most books on organisational change are aimed solely at leaders and managers, those traditionally seen as the ones in the driving seat. While school leaders will no doubt be the primary audience of this book, our approach is slightly different: this book is for everyone. Whether you are a teacher developing young minds, a parent supporting your child with homework, an HR manager grappling with a teacher recruitment and retention crisis, or the CEO of a multinational school group trying to leverage the power of a network, there is something here for you. Our aim is to broaden the perception of who holds the power to create change, and how to share it. We encourage you to let go of identities and what our 'roles' mean. If you find this book helpful, or think it could benefit your team, your community, or someone else entirely, please share it. We invite you to rethink your culture and shift from seeking perceived stability to engaging in long-term, real, and impactful conversation.

DOI: 10.4324/9781003596141-1

Change Starts Here

The word *change* and its association can come across as exciting, but what we don't speak about is the pain of change. Yes, change involves adopting something new but at the same time it often requires letting go of part of our current identity, a part that we've become deeply familiar and comfortable with.

Perceptions of Change

In the places where it is talked about, the word 'change' has developed a negative connotation, leading to the perception that change is inherently bad. As a result, many organisations now avoid using the term 'change' altogether, opting instead for more positive words such as 'innovation'. When writing this book, we considered adapting our language to use a word that may be more widely accepted. However, we ultimately decided against it, as the concept we are discussing is, in fact, change.

It is our belief that change should not be viewed as something scary or intimidating. This is precisely why we have been intentional about using the word 'change' throughout this book, as we aim to reframe the conversation and encourage a more open and positive approach to the concept of change.

This requires feeling safe with risk, despite the pressures. Without a strong sense of who we are and how this change aligns with our identity, change can feel 'over there', disconnected from us as humans. This feeling is especially strong when we consider significant changes: if we don't feel secure enough to be vulnerable and have important conversations, it's only natural to cling to the familiar for perceived security, even if it's not ideal.

The challenge is how to create an environment where people feel safe exploring change together, as leaders, teachers, parents, and individuals, through meaningful dialogue and reflection. How do we have difficult conversations that allow us to recognise what we have that's good and also grow together in facing the new and unknown?

Every stakeholder in education has the power to influence change, and recognising this is our first step. Decisions can be made on behalf of people in order for change to occur, but if we truly value the input others can bring, the change will be better. Matthew Syed, a renowned author and thinker on high performance and mindset, believes that incorporating feedback and insights from a diverse range of people leads to more effective decision-making and innovation, what he calls collective intelligence.[1] By embracing this collective intelligence, we can create more effective and lasting solutions. It will last due to the impact of everyone being involved, and it will allow future change to be more frequent and natural, making it sustainable.

Definition: Stakeholders

Commonly Used Meaning

The term 'stakeholders' has roots in business, initially describing anyone with an interest or 'stake' in a company's outcomes, including employees, customers, and investors. However, 'stakeholders' can feel somewhat detached, as if people are passive onlookers rather than active contributors.

What We Mean

We use 'stakeholders' to describe all those who play a direct, essential role in achieving shared goals. Far from being passive, stakeholders are critical participants who actively shape the organisation's direction. This term acknowledges their importance as partners rather than participants.

Change Starts Here

It is perhaps this liberating idea that also constricts us. If anyone can leverage change, then our organisations become open to influence from a wide array of actors, both within and outside the organisation. This inclusivity is empowering, but it also introduces complexity. How do we move forward with change in such an unpredictable environment?

Our intention is not to create an academic tome or research paper. Instead, we offer a practical guide, posing questions that we've found helpful in our experience working with schools and organisations around the world. Our purpose is to encourage readers to consider change in a meaningful way, and, most importantly, to consider community-led change. Of course, the only reason we are able to approach these questions in this way is because of the groundwork laid by so many leaders in the coaching and leadership spheres before us. It is thanks to their research and practical insight that we can present our book with confidence, knowing we stand on the shoulders of giants.

How do we ensure that the voices of many do not lead to chaos and confusion but instead to cohesive and effective change?

We aim to inspire a community-wide approach to change. One that seeks to value every voice, ensuring change is made by and for those most affected by it. These are the students, the teachers, the parents, and the school leaders. Notice we haven't mentioned the governments, the edu-companies, the consultants, or the influencers. While these players have important roles to play in supporting schools, the real benefit of their contributions comes when they complement a school-led vision. Meaningful change must come from within, from within the education community itself.

As we will explore throughout this book, each stakeholder plays a crucial role in shaping the future. Students bring fresh perspectives and needs that should be addressed. Teachers provide insights from the front lines. Parents offer valuable viewpoints on their children's development and wellbeing. School leaders have the strategic vision to guide institutions. By bringing all these voices together, we can create a more inclusive, effective approach to change.

The importance of values in driving change cannot be overstated. As the Common Cause Foundation[2] advocate, our values represent our guiding principles and broadest motivations, influencing our attitudes and behaviours in profound ways. Values have been shown to impact everything from our political persuasions to our ecological footprints and feelings of personal wellbeing.

When it comes to organisational change, understanding and leveraging values is a powerful tool. Rather than focusing solely on external incentives or rational arguments, we need to tap into the intrinsic motivations that drive people. By aligning our change efforts with values like universalism (understanding and protecting the welfare of all people and nature) and benevolence (preserving and enhancing the welfare of people close to us), we can create more meaningful and sustainable transformations.

What follows is a roadmap to understand your change, regardless of your role within it. We will help you recognise your power to influence change and show you how to harness it effectively.

Whether you are initiating change or responding to it, it is our hope that we equip you with powerful questions that support you in the powerful work you do.

Organisational Change Is Complex

Read that again. Change is complex.

Anyone who tells you otherwise is oversimplifying. And there are a lot of people who promote this idea. We've read the websites, seen the sales models, and dredged through the change frameworks. You must have heard it too: follow our process, do these things, complete this analysis, recruit our services, all with the promise that your change will have the impact you want. But this misses the basic fact of change: it is complex. Even the simplest changes are complex. Let's consider this one.

A school wants to improve reading in Lower Primary. They choose a supplier who has approached them with a phonics programme. This programme has been shown in other schools to boost reading scores, so the school buys the programme and books, and implements the training. What could possibly go wrong? Well here's a few places it could.

Perhaps students, like Emily and Abu, are already making great progress with the current reading instruction method, and switching to the new programme disrupts their learning.

Perhaps teachers, such as Ms Thompson and Mr Carter, are accustomed to another programme and have expertise in that approach, leading to resistance and lack of enthusiasm for the new one.

Perhaps there aren't enough books and materials for the phonics programme, meaning students like Sophie and Ethan don't have the required materials for practice at home.

Perhaps parents, like Mr Li, might not support the new phonics approach, believing it isn't the best method for their children.

Perhaps the school overestimates the programme's impact based on other schools' results, leading to disappointment for Principal Jones when the expected improvements don't materialise.

Perhaps the time required for the programme's full implementation is underestimated, leaving teachers like Mr Brown feeling rushed and unprepared.

Perhaps the programme doesn't address underlying issues, such as the socio-economic challenges faced by students like Alex and Maria, affecting their ability to benefit from the new method.

Perhaps unrealistic expectations set by the programme's promotional materials lead to disappointment for teachers like Ms Evans when the promised dramatic improvements take much longer to manifest.

This is not intended as a negative call to action, but it demonstrates a point. Change is complex, and one thing makes it so: a human is the most complex entity we know – and that's just one. Now imagine several working together.

Humans Are Messy

Humans are at the heart of organisational change, creating a complexity of almost incomprehensible scale. Organisations by their nature are complex. They are shaped by a unique set of values, vision, people, and culture, foundations that shape their identity and influence long-term success. The challenge is to anchor these foundations in a culture that is ready for change and innovation. Organisations must innovate to stay competitive and meet evolving stakeholder needs. Edgar Schein defines organisational culture as shared assumptions, values, and beliefs that influence interactions and work.[3] Culture, which manifests in visible structures and deeply embedded assumptions, shapes organisational identity and effectiveness. These assumptions guide behaviour and decision-making within an organisation, making culture a key predictor of success.

John Kotter, a renowned expert on change management, also highlights an important point about the nature of change.[4] He argues that the issue is not simply that change is complex, but rather that even when change initiatives are successful, they sometimes fail to last. It's not enough to see positive results in the short term; we must also focus on embedding the change into the very fabric of our organisations. This means integrating it into our daily operations, our culture, and our values. Otherwise, we risk seeing our hard-won progress unravel over time. Old habits and practices resurface, undoing the progress we've made. Organisational culture can make meaningful change and adaptation increasingly difficult as long-standing practices and group dynamics may resist new approaches and innovations.[5] From rigid systems to deep-rooted cultures, internal inertia makes the path to change daunting.

Another important consideration is the inherent value of people within our organisations. This is why the work we are doing feels so deeply personal. Our book aims to shift the perception of individuals' roles and contributions. Each person has genuine value, regardless of their position. They bring different perspectives, unique skill sets, and the ability to nurture these relationships that are essential to organisational success.

However, while people can be our most valuable resource, they can also be our most complex and potentially detrimental asset. The same qualities that make individuals invaluable, such as their diverse viewpoints and unique talents, can also introduce conflict. Facing these complexities directly is crucial to bring out the full potential of every member within the organisation.

Definition: Resource

Commonly Used Meaning

Referring to people as 'resources' has become standard in organisations, but it often feels impersonal, reducing individuals to mere assets or tools for achieving goals. This terminology can create a sense of detachment, where the unique contributions of people are overlooked.

What We Mean

When we use 'resource' in this context, we aim to recognise the skills, knowledge, and energy each individual brings. While 'resource' is a practical term, we strive to use it with respect, understanding that each person is much more than a 'resource': they are integral, valued contributors whose insights and talents shape the organisation.

Team Dynamics

Multiple team membership adds another layer to our change land-scape. As Sam Crome discusses in *The Power of Teams*,[6] most of us belong to several teams at once – perhaps a subject department, pasto-ral team, research group, or coaching partnership. Each of these teams operates differently, with its own purpose and ways of working.

When we change how one team works, we're not just affecting that isolated group. The impact ripples through to every other team where our colleagues are members. Traditional structures like subject depart-ments still matter, yet schools increasingly work through fluid arrange-ments that don't fit neatly into organisational charts. This means we need to think carefully about how change in one team might create tension or opportunities in others.

What looks like resistance to change might actually be someone trying to balance competing demands from their different teams. Understanding these connections helps us make change work rather than getting stuck in silos.

The Common Cause Foundation[7] highlight the importance of under-standing values and how they dynamically interact, which can lead to unintended consequences. These are known in medicine as iatro-genic effects and are incredibly relevant to education. For instance, in education, implementing a new strategy aimed at improving student learning might inadvertently increase staff workload. This can lead to teacher burnout, despite the strategy's well-intentioned goals.

In light of all of this, it may be fair to say that a perfect change pro-cess can never exist. We certainly believe so. But we need something to follow.

We believe that it starts by asking powerful questions and creating a space for these questions to resonate. But before we look at what questions we need to ask, we should first explore why a new approach is needed at all.

Resonance

We live in a world that often encourages compartmentalisation, neatly separating people, departments, and ideas into distinct categories. While this can help simplify complexity and improve efficiency, it only addresses part of the picture. In *The Fifth Discipline*,[8] Peter Senge, a pioneer of systems thinking, shows that meaningful transformation happens when we look beyond the parts to the connections between them, how they interact, overlap, and influence one another. As we explored in the context of organisational change, it's the potential in these connections, the space in-between, where lasting organisational change can occur.

> ## Definition: Streamline
>
> ### Commonly Used Meaning
>
> 'Streamline' has its roots in engineering, where it refers to reducing friction and improving efficiency. In organisations, the term often describes efforts to make processes faster or more cost effective, sometimes prioritising immediate results over sustainable improvements.
>
> ### What We Mean
>
> Streamlining means refining processes to ensure they are clear, efficient, and aligned with organisational goals. While speed and efficiency are important, the focus is on developing work-flows that are smooth, consistent, and effective. By building on existing practices, streamlining drives long-term improvements without compromising quality or purpose.

This book is an invitation to begin a conversation about that space.

While the voices of students, teachers, parents, and school leaders are each powerful in their own right, the real impact comes when those voices connect and resonate with one another. It's in the relationships, the shared efforts, and the dialogue that change is truly born and sustained.

'One person can carry one, whereas two people can carry three.' This simple proverb highlights the extraordinary synergy that happens when people work together. It's in this space, between what we contribute individually and what we create collectively, that something far greater emerges.

Resonance, at its core, is about amplification. The term *resonates* originates from physics, specifically relating to sound waves. When something resonates, it means that sound waves are being amplified, reverberating, and creating a deeper, more lasting impact. In the same way, Otto Scharmer, in *Theory U*, explains how resonance in human interactions builds collective presence and can lead to transformative change.[9]

Resonance means that our actions, ideas, and efforts build upon each other, creating a greater collective impact than what could be achieved individually. This resonance allows the energy of a single idea or action to multiply, much like the way sound waves strengthen as they reverberate through a space. It is this amplification and collective energy that we seek to nurture in educational environments.

However, resonance is not just external, it also happens internally within each of us. Internal resonance refers to how our beliefs, values, and experiences align, creating a sense of coherence that helps us experience change more effectively. When individuals experience internal resonance, they are more likely to engage authentically and contribute meaningfully to collective efforts. This internal alignment amplifies their ability to connect with others and contribute to a shared vision. Therefore, meaningful resonance starts with a deep internal connection that extends outward, allowing individuals to harmonise their contributions with those around them, ultimately leading to a stronger, more unified effort.

Definition: Alignment

Commonly Used Meaning

'Alignment' originates from the concept of arranging things in a straight line, commonly applied in technical or military contexts. In the organisational world, it often refers to ensuring that teams or individuals are 'in line' with a central vision or strategy. However, alignment can sometimes imply rigid conformity, as if people are expected to adopt the same viewpoints without room for individuality.

What We Mean

In our context, alignment is about fostering genuine connection to a shared direction. It's not about erasing differences but about creating a foundation where individual perspectives contribute to a common goal. We see alignment as a collaborative effort, where everyone's unique strengths are respected and channelled towards a cohesive vision.

In organisations, and particularly in education, we often focus on improving individual roles or departments, believing that change will come by strengthening each part in isolation. But the true power of change lies in the interplay between those parts, in the overlaps, and in the moments of shared action. As Margaret Wheatley suggests in *Leadership and the New Science*, leadership thrives in networks of cooperation rather than isolated, siloed structures.[10] Just as the brain's neural networks rely on the connections between different regions, communities and organisations thrive on the relationships that form between people, ideas, and experiences.

This space in-between is where the richest, most complex dynamics unfold, yet it is often overlooked. We tend to focus so much on the parts that we miss the power of the whole. Throughout this book, we invite you to explore how to engage with that space, how to embrace the complexity, the diversity, and the sometimes messy process of collaboration. As you reflect on your role in the changes around you, remember to engage with others, build connections, and bridge gaps in that space in-between.

Resonance can occur when we intentionally create a space that cultivates comfort and acceptance of the change process. This involves crafting an environment where opportunities and thoughtful questions encourage open dialogue and reflection, helping to deepen collective understanding. While resonance can arise in many ways, designing spaces that facilitate both agreement and the challenges of differing perspectives can amplify connection.

True progress also requires embracing dissonance, those moments of discomfort and differing opinions, as opportunities for learning and meaningful dialogue. Resonance, while powerful, can sometimes mask necessary dissonance, leading to complacency and stifling growth. Effective change demands that we balance resonance with dissonance. Adam Grant, in *Think Again*, underscores the value of using moments of friction to drive deeper understanding and create more inclusive solutions.[11] In the relationship between resonance and dissonance, we find the richest opportunities for meaningful, sustained change.

A Confidence Crisis

School leadership and community confidence is at an all-time low. Our contention is that one of the core reasons for this is autonomy:

autonomy of decisions but also autonomy of knowledge. This is supported by multiple studies, including a prominent study in the UK showing that teacher autonomy has a direct correlation with teacher satisfaction and retention.[12]

When teachers and leaders lack autonomy, their sense of ownership and investment in the change process can significantly decline. Autonomy, the ability to make choices and have a voice in decision-making, is crucial for fostering engagement and commitment to change initiatives. Without it, teachers and leaders may feel like mere executors of top-down directives, leading to decreased job satisfaction and a lack of motivation. For Daniel Pink,[13] autonomy is the desire to direct our own lives and work, and is a key driver of engagement and performance.

This links closely to self-efficacy, the confidence of educators to fulfil their duties. Confidence is also at an all-time low. Leaders we speak to consistently discuss their uncertainty in decision-making. Add this to a fast-changing world (consider the recent boom of Generative AI), and it's a perfect storm. You would assume that in an era of rapid change, organisations would be in a prime position to lead and innovate. Established solutions may not work, especially those solutions and systems that haven't changed in so long, so it would fall to organisations to drive change forward. However, it seems we actually face the opposite.

This vacuum has initially been filled with voices outside the school corridors, namely in three areas: policy, companies, and consultants. Let's tackle each of those three.

Firstly, there is increasing pressure on schools from policymakers and system-level leadership. This is partly normal practice: governments know that education is a key determinant of a stable and successful society. But it is also a form of organisational control. In the UK, for example, many schools have now formed part of large networks of multi-academy trusts. These trusts bring together schools, and one would assume they are simply a net positive. Who wouldn't want increased collaboration and economies of scale for schools? The same has happened in international schools, with over a quarter of international schools globally now being owned by big school groups. While the benefits are clear, there is also the risk that centralisation means less autonomy for school leaders; decisions may be made more at a group level. Not only this, but often leaders may delegate some of their responsibilities upwards to a manager (e.g., a regional professional development lead). This can mean that expertise is not held within the school where day-to-day decisions are made.

Added to this, we have a sector full of private industry and enterprise. For this book, we make the assumption that companies and organisations are, for the most part, very well intentioned and eager to support schools with innovative ideas. But the sheer number of products and scale of solutions offered to schools is overwhelming. Add to that a never-ending list of consultants, and there are endless ways you can involve external actors in your organisation. The challenge is not the existence of these external players but ensuring their work complements and strengthens the internal capacity of schools, rather than unintentionally replacing it.

Codification

In recent years, education has seen a marked shift towards codification. Teaching practices, leadership models, and professional learning structures have been meticulously broken down into frameworks and guidelines. While codification simplifies complex tasks, making them more accessible and easier to replicate, it often overlooks the crucial role of context.

Context lives in the space between the codes. It may not always be visible in the polished graphics or tidy explanations, yet it profoundly influences how education unfolds in reality. While codification provides clarity, we must remain vigilant not to overlook the nuances that context brings. Each educational environment is unique, shaped by its own set of challenges and opportunities. Recognising and valuing this context ensures that our approaches remain flexible and responsive to the needs of those we aim to serve.

A Cumulative Effect

The problem? This is causing a slow death of organisational confidence in schools. More and more, schools are outsourcing their thinking to external organisations. This has a cumulative effect: each time an external player makes a decision or drives change within a school, valuable knowledge is lost about how to deliver these outcomes internally. We are gradually handing over our knowledge, skills, and experience to players who, no matter how well intentioned and experienced, cannot know our schools as intimately as we do. This isn't about critiquing external support but about recognising that it works best when it complements and strengthens the expertise and confidence already present within the school community, rather than overshadowing or replacing it. While external solutions may lead to short-term improvements, they are unlikely to create the sustainable, deeply rooted change that schools truly need.

In turn, this can lead to the self-efficacy of school leaders diminishing as change is fleeting and excellence is unstable. Our only way forward is to re-empower school communities to drive change from the inside out. We do that by only engaging with the outside when our school community fully understands its purpose. This is the starting point for this book and is best summarised by Powell and Kusuma-Powell[14] who said rightly,

It's all about reclaiming our profession.

The Solution: A Process Guided by Questions and Community

We recognise the inferred irony of this book. A book that aims to help you bring power back to your school by giving you yet another model to do it. But there is a difference. This is not a prescriptive model. You won't find a clear how-to guide here. We make no assumptions about your context. Instead, we offer questions. Questions for you to reflect on, both on your own and with your community. Questions open up possibility. Statements restrict our reality.

Nuance matters. Rarely is there a single answer or absolute truth. Questions can invite us to pause and consider the layers beneath the surface, creating space to explore what might otherwise remain hidden. They can help us anchor ourselves in the moment, making room for subtleties and perspectives we might have overlooked. In this way, questions don't only open up possibilities, they open space for conversations, offering a chance to connect and discover together.

There are different types of questions, and understanding their purpose can help shape meaningful conversations. Coaching questions, as Michael Bungay Stanier explores in *The Coaching Habit*,[15] serve a purpose beyond leading someone to a particular answer. The point of a good coaching question is to be genuinely curious, free from hidden agendas. It invites exploration without assumption, values the other person's experience, and avoids simply turning a statement into a question by adding a question mark at the end. In contrast, 'why' questions often make people defensive, implying judgement or requiring justification. They can close doors, whereas coaching questions should open them.

Just because we ask a question doesn't mean it isn't leading somewhere, but when we ask thoughtfully and with genuine curiosity, the destination is shared understanding, not an answer we have already chosen. Questions also have layers; given time and space, even the same question can take on new meaning. They allow us to build trust, empathy, and clarity together, helping us see the potential that statements alone cannot provide.

There are four key advantages to question-driven organisational change involving the whole community.

1. The quality of the change is better as it considers and values multiple perspectives.

2. There is genuine buy-in and promotion because we transform our organisation from passive recipients of instructions to change, to ambassadors for change who actively promote it.
3. It lasts, allowing our organisation to feel safe with change again and to share more openly, encouraging future change.
4. Questions encourage us to connect with our feelings, not just with the head, but with the heart, which will help us follow through with a change.

Definition: Buy-in

Commonly Used Meaning

'Buy-in' originated as a financial term for purchasing an investment. In organisations, it's used to describe gaining support for an idea or project, often implying that people must be persuaded to 'buy into' a concept, almost as if it were a product to be sold.

What We Mean

For us, buy-in is not about persuading people but about creating a vision that resonates with them. True buy-in is built on a foundation of shared values, where people feel a sense of personal investment in the organisation's goals. It reflects genuine commitment, and garners support because it aligns with their own values and purpose.

A question-based approach encourages open conversation and creates opportunities for you and your community to develop clear, internal confidence when engaging with the world. This model advocates for leadership that comes from within, enabling your organisation to drive change authentically and organically, rather than relying solely on leaders or external forces.

This approach involves the entire community: teachers, support staff, parents, students, and local stakeholders. Questions are designed to evoke thoughtful dialogue, allowing you to guide the conversation in a way that reflects your unique needs, rather than steering toward predetermined outcomes or ideas.

Another key purpose of this approach is to minimise the HiPPO effect (Highest Paid Person's Opinion), a concept popularised by Avinash Kaushik.[16] This effect demonstrates how we often look to the highest paid person first in our collaboration. Reducing this effect requires bringing the community in early and safely, creating a space where no single voice dominates simply due to perceived authority. While HiPPO often refers to the highest paid person, it can also apply to anyone in the community, be it a leader, parent, staff member, or student, who holds disproportionate social influence or is seen as having more knowledge. Though it can be difficult to fully neutralise this imbalance, consciously asking questions that involve the entire community can bring to the surface unspoken perspectives that significantly impact the group.

Matthew Syed says that cognitive diversity, the inclusion of different viewpoints, backgrounds, and experiences, actually enables groups to tackle complex problems more effectively.[17] Without this, organisations risk 'collective blindness', where dominant voices or assumptions limit the group's potential. By using an inclusive questioning approach, we create space for these diverse ideas to surface, helping to prevent narrow thinking and opening up new possibilities that might otherwise remain hidden.

So where do we ask these questions? The environment plays a significant role by shaping discussions, whether it's influenced by leaders, group dynamics, or the presence of limiting beliefs. These questions can be explored both in groups and individually, offering you opportunities for collective insight as well as personal reflection. In groups, they can help to dismantle groupthink and challenge dominant voices, while individually, they allow space to deeply consider personal biases or assumptions that may go unnoticed in larger discussions.

The key is to be mindful of your context. Only you truly understand the dynamics of your organisation or community, and you're best positioned to determine when and where these questions will have the most impact. Whether in formal meetings, casual conversations, or private moments of reflection, these questions are flexible tools that can be adapted to fit your unique situation.

Not all questions need to be answered, and certainly not immediately. Questions themselves create an opportunity for exploration. Because they aren't rigid or set, we can become more comfortable with the unknown, acknowledging that 'not knowing' is perfectly okay, and sometimes even necessary. As Voltaire famously said, 'Judge a man by his questions rather than by his answers'.

The Coaching Conundrum

As we consider how to support change in schools, coaching inevitably enters the conversation. However, the current state of coaching in schools presents a peculiar challenge that warrants closer examination.

Unlike many organisations, schools tend to implement coaching in a fragmented way. At the top of the organisation, senior leaders often receive executive-style coaching, either funded by their organisation or privately secured. At the classroom level, teachers engage with instructional coaches to develop their practice. But between these two poles lies a vast middle ground where coaching is either absent or inconsistently applied.

Middle leaders, who often bear the weight of implementing change, rarely receive systematic coaching support. Parents, despite being crucial stakeholders in the educational journey, seldom experience coaching interactions. Some schools have ventured into student coaching, but approaches vary dramatically from one institution to another. This fragmentation creates a confused landscape where 'coaching' means different things to different people within the same organisation.

This inconsistency is particularly problematic when we consider the role coaching could play in organisational change. The power of coaching lies in its ability to start with questions rather than answers. Instead of presenting pre-packaged solutions, a coaching approach begins by understanding the context, challenges, and capabilities already present within the school community.

When we bring in external consultants or adopt new initiatives, the dynamic that often emerges can inadvertently centre around 'here's what we offer'. This isn't about fault or failure but reflects a dynamic that can arise when external support is introduced without a shared understanding of how it fits into the school's journey. At the same time, schools may not always be ready to articulate their needs or engage fully in this kind of partnership, which can unintentionally limit the effectiveness of the process. A more effective starting point might involve reframing the conversation: 'tell us about your journey' alongside 'here's how we can support you'. Such an approach creates space for a more meaningful exchange, ensuring that the process is rooted in the school's unique context while also allowing consultants to adapt their expertise accordingly. This shift from prescription to exploration aligns perfectly with our model of change, where connection and discovery precede action. Organisational coaching, when implemented systematically across all levels of the school, can create the conditions for more authentic and sustainable change.

The key is to move away from fragmented coaching interventions towards a more cohesive, school-wide coaching culture. This means extending coaching beyond its traditional domains and thinking about how coaching conversations can support all stakeholders in the change process.

The Double Diamond

So if questions are our best bet, which ones should we be asking, who should we be asking them to, and in what order? This is where a model helps. We have followed the open-source spirit of the British Design Council. Their design model, although predominantly not used in education, is an excellent and simple framework to attach questions to in the process of change.

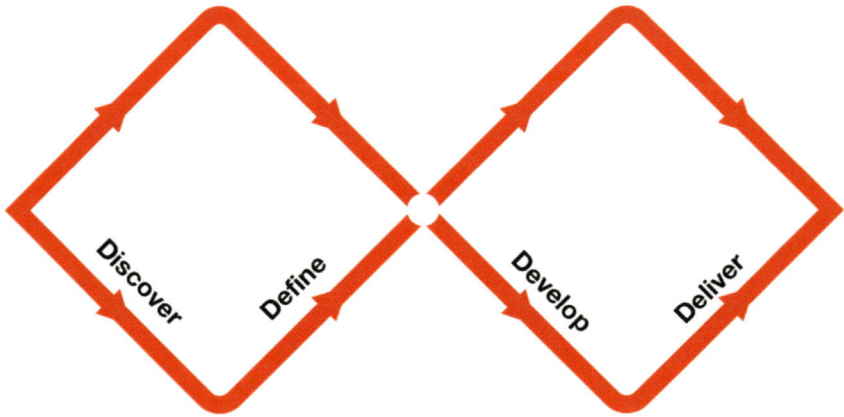

British Design Council, 2015[18]

We were drawn to this model for its simplicity but more so for its ability to promote a culture of exploration and thinking, something that we perhaps don't get the opportunity to do in the day-to-day.

The model starts at the left and purposely expands outward in the Discover stage, exploring whether the original issue is really the issue that needs a solution. After that, the model contracts in the Define stage, coming to the middle point where you have a clearly defined problem to solve. This initiates the second stage of exploration as we go wide again and develop solutions, followed by a contraction for delivery. Our model for organisational change is based on this simple model and expands upon it, specifically making it more people-centric.

Although it may seem linear, this process is ultimately a cycle. Yes, there is an endpoint for this specific change but the key is not in the change alone but rather the ability to feel safe to listen, share, and innovate. A great success for this model is not in the endpoint but rather in the improved ability and willingness to start this process over next time.

What follows is a short explanation of how you can use this book followed by a detailed breakdown of our model for organisational change. Keep in mind that the model is less important than the questions. This model is meant to be played with.

How to Use This Book

Firstly, we have made an assumption. One that we feel pretty safe to make. That is you already have immense wisdom. You have skills. You have experience. You are not a blank sheet of paper. This is the failing of many self-help or change books you might read; they assume you are starting from scratch. It would be hypocritical of us to label a book 'Change Starts Here' and then assume that 'here' is an empty vessel. That's not the point. The point is that you, your school, and your community already have the knowledge you need to succeed. As such, you should approach this book as an assistant to help you do your best thinking, not a guidebook that will tell you how to execute your change in detail.

First, here's a breakdown of what you will find on the following pages, followed by some suggestions on how you might read the rest of the book.

The Model (page 26)

We give you an overview of our model for organisational change. Here you will get to know the double diamond design in more detail. We provide an explanation of why each step is important and how you should frame conversations within it. If you are an experienced coach, you might wish to stop here and use the model to inspire your own questioning. However, we have provided some powerful questions in the following sections that will make this easier.

Stories (page 33)

Context is everything. There's no point hearing an idea if you can't see it brought to life. To exemplify the process, we have provided four real-world case studies: You will be introduced to the challenges faced by Alex, Mei, Taylor, and Jordan. These represent diverse perspectives in a school: a leader, a teacher, a parent, and a student. All of them are involved in change, and it is our hope that these examples will help you realise that the capacity to change doesn't only lie with leadership. With each section of the model for organisational change, we will provide examples of how each of these people responds to change.

40 Questions (page 38)

This is the bulk of the book and the section you will use the most. Here you will find 40 powerful yet simple questions that you can ask of yourself and your community. These questions are meant to be conversation starters: it is unlikely that you can have the most insightful conversation on your own. A conversation is, after all, communication between two or more humans. That is how you should use these questions.

Some of the questions are meant to be provocative; they should take you to a place of deep contemplation and allow for richer problem-solving. After each question, you will find a fuller explanation and rationale behind the question, including links to interesting studies, literature, and related case studies.

After every question we invite you to ask 'What else'.[19] The questions are only the start and you should not use them as the be-all-and-end-all of change. Use them to inspire further questions.

These questions will unlock change that is YOURS.

Reading Modes

Here are a few suggested reading modes to get you started. You will likely develop your own style.

What?	Who?	How?
The whole book	On your own	Reading on your own cover to cover is great if you want to ground yourself in the nature and complexity of change and the double diamond process.
	As a team	This book can work very well for a leadership team. Read the initial chapters together to ground yourself in the overall thinking. Then choose a perceived challenge you are facing and go through the questions in order, provoking your thinking as you go. If it is your first time, choose something simple and see where it takes you.
Independent chapters	On your own	You may be at an inflection moment which brought you to this book – something you are stuck with. This is great. Find the chapter that matches where you are on the journey and use the questions to unlock your own thinking and next steps.
	As a team	Perhaps your inflection moment is one identified by the team. Great. Open the book together at the place you are at with your change and ask the questions of yourself to see where it takes you.
Online Support		At any point, head to workcollaborative.com to explore templates, group activity ideas, an online community, and research to support your change.

You will notice that, even though each part of the double diamond has five associated questions, it will take different amounts of time to go through each stage. They are not intended to be equal. In addition, we are not going to tell you which should take longer and shorter. Why? Because this depends on your context. If you have a school where you identify low levels of trust within the team, then it is likely that the first part of the double diamond will take you a long time. In the same way, if the goal you choose to pursue requires a fundamental shift to 'the way things work around here', then it is likely that your second diamond is going to take more time. The complexity and individuality of your change dictate the process, not the model itself.

Most challenges you encounter at a school will come at an inflection moment. This inflection moment may be right at the start of our process with a perceived challenge. But it could equally start at any point in the model. Therefore, don't think you have to start from scratch with every inflection moment; instead, reflect on where you are experiencing the challenge on the double diamond, and jump to the questions in that section. The very fact you are reading this book hints that you are not at zero.

And remember, the aim of this book is not to point fingers at what you haven't done, but to dig deeply into a rigorous, purposeful, and community-led change. Good luck!

Organisational Change Model

So here it is, yet another model . . .

We see the irony. This is another book to help you, and we frame it around a model. What makes this different?

We're going to tell you something that might seem counter-intuitive but there's intention in this request. Use this model not as an instruction manual but rather as a guide to connecting more meaningfully with your community through this process. Only you will understand the context needed for this.

We are not here to tell you to follow our model in every detail with fidelity. We're not even here to tell you to follow the model at all. Instead, we provide a model that acts as a framework to ask yourself those powerful questions.

We have adapted the model from the double diamond design. This adaptation speaks to the fact that organisations are different from products. At its core, this is about people. And as we have stated, people are complex. Because of this, we have enhanced the model to respond to the beautiful complexity of human interaction in change.

Adapted from The Double Diamond by the Design Council (licensed under a CC BY 4.0 licence)

The model consists of eight key stages, each of which includes five questions for you to think about in the subsequent chapters. These stages are punctuated at three points: the challenge, goal, and solution. Here, we will outline each of the stages, including why this change is in the model and what the aim of each stage is. You will notice that each stage is grouped into pairs. This is due to their overlapping nature. One does not come after the other; instead, they are intended to be addressed simultaneously. All of the questions in the first diamond are about exploring the challenge as a community. The second diamond is about solving that challenge as a community. Community is at the heart of this process. It is not a model to be confined to the ranks of senior leadership teams. It will not work if that is your intention.

Remember, this model is not only about this one change. It is about building a foundation for successful and sustainable future change. It is about culture. Keep coming back to these questions. The work is never done.

Our model for organisational change also recognises the critical role that values play in shaping behaviours and attitudes. As we move through the stages of Connect, Discover, Define, and beyond, we must continually reflect on how our change efforts are engaging with people's core values. Are we appealing to intrinsic motivations like self-direction and universalism? Or are we inadvertently reinforcing extrinsic values like power and achievement that may undermine long-term change?

The Common Cause Foundation's research shows that prioritising intrinsic values is closely related to behaviours like political engagement, concern about social justice, and environmentally friendly actions. By consciously cultivating these values throughout our change process, we can create a stronger foundation for lasting transformation. This may mean rethinking how we communicate, structure our organisations, and design policies to ensure they embody the values we wish to promote.

And we could be wrong; this is why we have made our model open source. You can read it, play with it, chop it up, and do with it what you will. All we ask is that you share what you do. That is the spirit of open source.

We have purposely decided to release this model at an early stage. The model will grow and adapt as more people use it. You may even challenge the research. This is great.

Here is a quick breakdown of the process. At the start of the question chapters you will find a more detailed breakdown.

Sponsor's Perceived Challenge

The change process within a school begins with a perceived challenge or opportunity identified by an individual or group, like a teacher, leader, or even parents. These are the sponsors of the change. This initial perception may not necessarily represent the actual challenge faced by the school, but it serves as the starting point for the change process. It is essential that the perceived challenge is subject to further exploration and refinement as the process unfolds, taking into account the needs of the school community.

Connect

Building a foundation of trust and psychological safety within the school community is crucial for effective change to occur. This step focuses on connection: creating an environment where teachers, staff, students, and parents feel comfortable sharing their thoughts, ideas, and concerns. Without a strong foundation of trust and psychological safety, the change process may face significant obstacles and resistance, as stakeholders may be hesitant to engage in open and honest dialogue about the challenges and opportunities facing the school.

Discover

This expansive stage involves exploring the challenge from multiple perspectives, considering the thoughts and experiences of various stakeholders within the school community, and determining if it is the real challenge that needs to be addressed. The team should engage in a wide-ranging exploration, gathering insights from teachers, students, parents, and other stakeholders, and examining the challenge in the context of the school's mission, values, and goals. This stage helps to ensure that the team is focusing on the most relevant and impactful issues affecting the school and its community.

Define

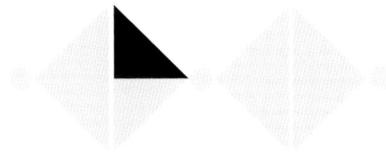

After generating ideas and gathering input from the school community, the team narrows down the focus to the specific challenge they want to tackle and creates a shared vision for the future of the school. This step involves synthesising the information gathered during the Discover stage and reaching a consensus on the primary challenge to address. By defining a clear vision and setting goals, the team establishes a common purpose and direction for the change process, ensuring that all are working towards the same objectives for the school's improvement.

Align

Alignment across all stakeholders within the school community, including teachers, leaders, parents, students, and support staff, is essential for effective change. Engaging and involving everyone in the change process helps to build buy-in, understanding, and commitment to the shared vision and goals for the school. Alignment ensures that everyone is working towards the same objectives and minimises potential resistance or conflicting priorities, which can be particularly challenging in a school setting where stakeholders often have diverse perspectives.

Community Defined Goal

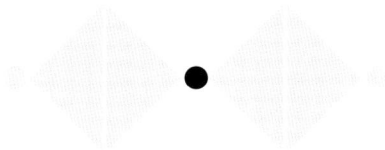

This brings you to the shared goal, clearly defined and ready to tackle. You are in a much stronger position now to move forward than when it was simply a perceived challenge owned by one person.

Develop

Change Starts Here

In this expansive stage, the team explores potential solutions to achieve the goal, identifies knowledge gaps, and seeks external support if needed to address the specific challenges facing the school. The team should brainstorm and consider a wide range of solutions, evaluating their feasibility, impact, and alignment with the school's mission, values, and goals.

Learn

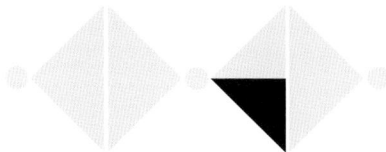

In this stage, the team actively seeks opportunities to acquire the necessary knowledge and skills to successfully implement the chosen solution(s). The team identifies knowledge gaps and engages in targeted learning activities, such as professional development, research, collaboration with experts, or partnerships with other schools. Building the capacity and expertise of the team is essential to ensure that they are well equipped to lead and manage the change process effectively.

Deliver

The team selects the most promising solution and implements this through a well-defined delivery process. This step involves careful planning, resource allocation, and project management to ensure the successful execution of the chosen solution within the school. The delivery process should be well documented, with clear roles, responsibilities, and timelines established to facilitate smooth implementation, taking into account the unique schedules, curricula, and needs of the school and its community.

Sustain

To ensure long-term success and adaptability, the team establishes habits and tactics to maintain the implemented changes. Sustaining change requires ongoing effort, monitoring, and adjustment to ensure that the new practices and behaviours become embedded in the school's culture.

Stories

In each section, we have included stories that represent people we've met and worked with: students, families, school leaders, and teachers who have all experienced challenges with change. The purpose of including these stories is to bring to life how this change model has allowed us to see change in our own practice and how it can improve change for our organisations to be both qualitatively and quantitatively better, empowering everyone involved so the culture around the change lasts well into the future.

Having a personal account can also make it easier for you, the reader, to connect with these ideas. We aim to include these people and their stories to show you how change is possible and how important it can be to bring your organisation and school community into the process.

You see, we could provide only research, we could offer ideas and theories, but that isn't the aim; this isn't an academic tome or a reference book. Instead, it is the wealth of existing research, the books we reference throughout, that enables us to present these ideas in a more accessible way. The aim of this book is to serve as a practical guide, with practical and thought-provoking questions that you can ask in your organisation to think about how change can matter to you and the impact that may have on every individual within your school community.

Let's introduce you to each of their perceived challenges.

Alex

Alex is a parent of three, all of whom attend a primary school in the local town. Alex and his partner recently separated, which has meant that Alex has had to move further away from the area where the children go to school.

He and his ex-partner share custody of the children, alternating weeks with them. The issue for Alex is that the children now have to travel an hour each way to school. Due to work commitments, Alex is unable to get them to and from school.

The school is highly sought after, known for its great holistic outcomes, and both Alex and his ex-partner don't want to take the children out of school. Alex needs to find a viable transport solution to get them to and from school and wants to seek support from the school.

You'll find out more about Alex's story in the Align and Sustain chapters.

Mei

Mei is an experienced history teacher in a small independent school. Mei always felt that teaching was her calling and is deeply connected to the fact she is helping the next generation, especially having come from a family of teachers.

Mei is feeling frustrated currently because she feels like she's constantly having to replan her lessons and schemes of work. She feels like she hasn't got a connection to the other history teachers. They work in silos and keep their planning and resources to themselves; there's no shared bank of resources. She has a sense that others also share her frustration but they don't get much opportunity to raise their views.

She feels disconnected and frustrated that the school doesn't have a clear resource bank or curriculum that flows from teacher to teacher and year to year.

You'll hear more about Mei in the Discover and Develop chapters.

Taylor

Taylor was an 18-year-old student, popular among her peers and well-liked by teachers. Despite being outwardly confident, Taylor struggled with the pressures of exams, balancing her social life, and the lingering mental health impacts of the COVID-19 lockdowns.

Taylor often felt isolated and unsupported with her mental health and wellbeing. Although her school had some mental health programmes, they carried a stigma that deterred her from seeking help. She found herself longing for a safe space where she could openly discuss her challenges, especially regarding her future and feeling genuinely supported.

Taylor's perceived needs were clear: she craved a more personal approach to support for her mental health. She believed that mental wellbeing should be understood as deeply personal, not just a wellbeing tickbox. And her concerns extended beyond herself; she wanted her younger brother, Stephen, to grow up in a more supportive environment.

Taylor proposed a space for students to talk about their feelings openly and having a school counsellor available who was approachable and could offer confidential advice.

She planned to speak with the school leadership team about her ideas.

Change Starts Here

To follow Taylor's story, head to the Define and Learn chapters.

Jordan

Jordan is an experienced headteacher who recently took over as the Executive Headteacher of a large group of schools in the UK, commonly referred to as a Multi-Academy Trust (MAT). Having been in the role for almost two years, Jordan has worked tirelessly to ensure that both the financial and academic results meet high standards. When he inherited this role, he had no idea of the deep-seated problems in the schools across the group.

Jordan was initially unaware of the extent of the ongoing challenges the schools had faced over the years. He didn't realise how poor the academic results had been, or how disconnected the schools were from one another. It wasn't until he reviewed the recent inspection reports that he grasped the severity of the situation. Over the past two years, he has dedicated himself night and day to improving the MAT's position.

Despite these efforts, his biggest challenge remains the drop in student enrolment. Parents no longer want to send their children to the MAT, even though Jordan believes he has dramatically improved the schools since he joined. He believes that the key issue is communication: parents need to be informed about the significant improvements that have been made.

In Jordan's mind, once parents are aware, they will support the MAT and enrolment numbers will increase substantially.

Head to the Connect and Deliver chapters to explore Jordan's story

Notes

1 Syed, M. (2019). Rebel Ideas: *The Power of Diverse Thinking*. John Murray Press.

2 Common Cause Foundation. (2011). *The Common Cause Handbook.* https://commoncausefoundation.org/_resources/the-common-cause-handbook/

3 Schein, E. H. (2016). *Organizational Culture and Leadership* (5th ed.). Jossey-Bass.

4 Kotter, J. P. (2012). *Leading Change.* Harvard Business Review Press.

5 Lewin, K. (1947). Frontiers in group dynamics: Concept, method and reality in social science; social equilibria and social change. *Human Relations*, 1(1), 5–41.

6 Crome, S. (2024). *The Power of Teams: How to Create and Lead Thriving School Teams.* John Catt Educational.

7 Common Cause Foundation. (2011). *The Common Cause Handbook.* https://commoncausefoundation.org/_resources/the-common-cause-handbook/

8 Senge, P. M. (2006). *The Fifth Discipline: The Art and Practice of the Learning Organization* (rev. ed.). Currency/Doubleday.

9 Scharmer, C. O. (2016). *Theory U: Leading From the Future As It Emerges* (2nd ed.). Berrett-Koehler Publishers.

10 Wheatley, M. J. (2006). *Leadership and the New Science: Discovering Order in a Chaotic World* (3rd ed.). Berrett-Koehler Publishers.

11 Grant, A. (2021). *Think Again: The Power of Knowing What You Don't Know.* Penguin Random House.

12 Worth, J., & Van den Brande, J. (2020). *Teacher Autonomy: How Does It Relate to Job Satisfaction and Retention?* National Foundation for Educational Research. www.nfer.ac.uk

13 Pink, D. H. (2009). *Drive: The Surprising Truth About What Motivates Us.* Riverhead Books.

14 Powell, W., & Kusuma-Powell, O. (2015). *Teacher Self-Supervision: Why Teacher Evaluation Has Failed and What We Can Do About It.* John Catt Educational Ltd.

15 Bungay Stanier, M. (2016). *The Coaching Habit: Say Less, Ask More & Change the Way You Lead Forever.* Box of Crayons Press.

16 Kaushik, A. (2007). *Web Analytics: An Hour a Day.* Sybex.

17 Syed, M. (2019). *Rebel Ideas: The Power of Diverse Thinking.* John Murray Press.

18 British Design Council, 2015. www.designcouncil.org.uk/our-resources/framework-for-innovation. Licensed under a CC BY 4.0 license.

19 Bungay Stanier, M. (2016). *The Coaching Habit: Say Less, Ask More & Change the Way You Lead Forever.* Box of Crayons Press.

40
Questions

DOI: 10.4324/9781003596141-2

Sponsor's Perceived Challenge

PERCEIVED CHALLENGE — 1 — CONNECT DISCOVER — DEFINE ALIGN — COMMUNITY GOAL — 2 — DEVELOP LEARN — DELIVER SUSTAIN — SUSTAINED SOLUTION — 3

DOI: 10.4324/9781003596141-3

Change Starts Here

Before we start on our change journey, we must acknowledge a fundamental truth: every change has a sponsor. The sponsor is the initiator or initiators of the change, the person or group of people who first identify the issue and instigates the process.

And there is always a sponsor or sponsors.

We may think we arrive at decisions collaboratively, and sometimes we do, but there is always one person or a small group who strongly invests in the initial idea and pushes it forward. The sponsor is someone with influence, confidence (real or perceived), or power, someone who can initiate and drive change. In a school, this is almost always a leader, be it a department head or principal.

The sponsor's perceived challenge often arises from a deep sense of responsibility and a vision for improvement, prompting them to risk what feels safe and familiar. This individual or group feels the weight of maintaining the school's standards and sees an opportunity, or necessity, for change that aligns with their values and aspirations.

Their choice to act signals a willingness to stretch beyond their comfort zone, facing potential discomfort or uncertainty for the sake of growth. By initiating this journey, they seek to achieve meaningful progress, recognising that the potential outcomes, whether best or worst case, could reshape the future of their school community.

This marks an inflection moment, as Sharath Jeevan describes, a point where we must identify the 'asteroids' that could obstruct our progress and the 'starships' that could propel us forward.[1] Recognising these factors enables us to steer organisational change with clarity and intention, prioritising actions that secure immediate wins while laying a strong foundation for continuous, sustainable growth.

But in the rush to adapt, John Kotter and Holger Rathgeber[2] caution that there is a real risk of diluting the very identity and values that have driven the organisations' long-term success. Change always sits within a pre-developed culture.

For meaningful change to take root, Kurt Lewin[3] explains that there must first be an 'unfreezing', a collective acknowledgement of the need for change. This shared understanding sets the stage for the transition to unfold, allowing the shift to integrate into the organisation's culture and ultimately stabilise. We like this framing; before you start, ask yourself 'Am I willing to unfreeze my thinking?'

This may seem obvious, but the issue arises when we decide to take collaborative action. In our change model, we are moving towards a shared goal and shared solution. This means we want the change to be embraced by the entire community, not just the initial sponsor. All too often, however, a sponsor will articulate a 'challenge', the community will take on the role of implementation to respond to the challenge, and when they have implemented, it may not align with the sponsor's perception of the original challenge. This can lead to resistance and, at worst, a complete shut-down or U-turn, leading to resentment within the team. Speaking at people feels very different to working with them.

To avoid this, we start with the sponsor. Before embarking on a change project, the sponsor must accept the process ahead. As you can see from the double diamond model, the first diamond is all about establishing a community-aligned goal. This goal will inevitably differ from the initial perceived challenge. Therefore, our sponsor must recognise, and be willing to recognise, that their perceived problem may not be the actual problem and that the scope of the challenge may change.

This is essential.

Without this affirmation, you significantly reduce the likelihood of long-term success. In a top-down model, change may occur but will it last and what damage will that incur for the organisation's trust and connection? Openness is the first step. If you are a sponsor with a perceived challenge, can you accept that this is just your perception? Are you open to change? If not, this is not the process for you.

But if you are open, if you are willing to engage with your community to explore your perceived challenge with vulnerability and openness, you have taken your first significant step towards success. This unlocks the first step of the process: connect.

Notes

1 Jeevan, S. (2024). *Inflection: A Roadmap for Leaders at a Crossroads.* Intrinsic Press.
2 Kotter, J. P., & Rathgeber, H. (2006). *Our Iceberg Is Melting: Changing and Succeeding Under Any Conditions.* St. Martin's Press.
3 Lewin, K. (1947). Frontiers in group dynamics: Concept, method and reality in social science; social equilibria and social change. *Human Relations, 1*(1), 5–41.

Stage 1: Connect

PERCEIVED CHALLENGE

COMMUNITY GOAL

SUSTAINED SOLUTION

1

CONNECT DISCOVER

DEFINE ALIGN

2

DEVELOP LEARN

DELIVER SUSTAIN

3

DOI: 10.4324/9781003596141-4

Change Starts Here

You will notice that each triangle within the double diamond has two stages. This is purposeful. Often, we see change as a linear process, but it rarely is. We propose that you can indeed break down your change into four steps: the four triangles of the double diamond. However, within each of these are two steps that happen simultaneously. You may choose to try one before the other but it doesn't always work that way. So, we start with connect, but at the same time, you will also be discovering. Although connection is the focus here, connection is hopefully occurring throughout this entire process; it's not a standalone but there needs to be a conscious effort to start with.

The Connect stage is arguably the most important step for effective change as it forms the foundation of any successful transformation. Here, the aim is to gauge the current state of our organisation.

How are people feeling around here?

We want to gather information on people's perceptions of change, their assumptions about successful change, and the cultural dynamics of collaboration and trust in the school. We need to build these foundations before we journey too deep into change.

Building strong teams in schools requires more than just assembling a group of talented individuals. As Sam Crome shares in *The Power of Teams*, it's about creating a culture of belonging and psychological safety. This aligns closely with our focus on connection as a foundational element of change. When team members feel they truly belong and can trust those around them, they are more likely to engage fully in the change process, share ideas, and take risks. As leaders, we must prioritise creating an environment where every team member feels valued and heard, setting the stage for more effective collaboration and innovation.[1]

Remember, this is just one of many changes you will experience as a school. A strong foundation in this change will set you up for success in every subsequent change you undertake.

We've included five questions that allow you to both assess the current state of psychological safety and then engage in a discussion on how you can move it forward. Use this stage as a litmus test to check: are we ready for change? Are our foundations strong enough?

Trust us, it is worth staying here for a while.

Q1: When was the last time you felt truly heard?

Have you ever noticed that it's often in the most populated areas where we feel the most lonely? Our schools are no exception. Despite being surrounded by colleagues, the limited time available can make genuine listening and being heard a huge challenge.

The way we communicate shapes and affects our ability to connect. Many of us find ourselves speaking at each other rather than with each other, creating barriers to authentic sharing and understanding. And when we don't feel heard, it impacts our individual wellbeing, our work relationships and professional effectiveness. These communication patterns can significantly influence our organisations, particularly during times of change.

In the Connect stage, building strong relationships and trust is key. When people feel heard, they are more likely to engage meaningfully in the change process. However, the reality in many schools is that staff often withhold their thoughts, particularly when they have concerns about proposed changes. This silence can be costly. Valuable insights are lost, and potential problems remain unaddressed.

Embracing Discomfort

Change inherently requires stepping outside our comfort zone and embracing uncertainty. Without feeling connected, respected, and understood, commitment to change becomes fragile. The success of any change initiative depends heavily on including and valuing the perspectives of those it will affect.

Even with the best intentions, familiarity with close colleagues can lead to taking them for granted. We have to actively demonstrate that we value each person and their ideas, regardless of their role or title. This means creating space in our busy days to be fully present and attentive to others.

Change Starts Here

The question 'When was the last time you felt truly heard?' serves as a powerful gauge of our environment. Feeling heard is essential for psychological safety, a notion championed by Amy Edmonson,[2] and fosters belonging and trust. In the Connect stage, this foundation of trust becomes crucial. When people feel heard and valued, their work matters more deeply, creating a shared sense of ownership.

So how do you get to that place of better listening? The path lies in 'proactive inquiry', being genuinely curious, listening with empathy, and valuing what others share. As we create more space for others and show authentic interest in their perspectives, we strengthen our community's culture of connection.

It can be useful to remember that mechanisms are natural in professional settings. While self-protection is healthy, these barriers can prevent us from understanding each other and feeling safe enough to take risks, learn, and grow. The Connect stage focuses on carefully dismantling these barriers. As Jim Knight discusses in *Better Conversations*,[3] authentic connection requires alignment between who we claim to be and what we actually do. Authenticity can often be misunderstood as acting naturally, but this can easily slip from being thoughtful to thoughtless. In trust, being authentic is acting with intention and aligning our thoughts, actions, values, identity, and beliefs.

True authenticity enhances our connection with ourselves, others, and our shared community identity. By recognising where we might be closed off or inauthentic, we can identify and address barriers to genuine communication, whether they stem from time constraints, preconceived judgements, or lack of attention.

And while there will be times when urgent decisions must be made for us, regularly failing to listen to our community carries significant risks. The investment in listening pays dividends in stronger relationships, better decisions, and more effective implementation of change.

Q2: What happens when people make mistakes here?

Change Starts Here

The pressure to present perfection in schools is intense, particularly in a social-media driven world. But what we don't see behind the polished facades is the trial and error, the iterations, and yes, the mistakes. The way we handle mistakes, both individually and collectively, shapes the culture of our schools.

Creating space for mistakes requires a careful balance. The freedom to make mistakes signals a willingness to innovate and learn, yet how often do we truly feel comfortable making them? The instinct to hide our missteps, what Amy Edmondson[4] calls the 'Learning Trap', often feels safer than embracing accountability. However, this approach undermines the very foundation of trust we aim to build in the Connect stage.

Our response to mistakes, both our own and others', sends a powerful message about psychological safety within the organisation. Edmondson illustrates this through her concept of 'Blameless reporting' policies at children's hospitals and clinics:

> If we frame medical accidents as indications that someone screwed up, we will ignore or suppress them for fear of being blamed or of pointing the finger at a colleague. However, we can shift our automatic frames and create a shared frame that more accurately represents reality.[5]

This principle translates directly to schools. When organisations treat failures as opportunities for learning rather than blame, they create environments where innovation can flourish. Leaders play a crucial role here; their willingness to acknowledge their own mistakes sets the tone for the entire organisation. This openness builds trust and strengthens connections.

Matthew Syed's work on Black Box Thinking[6] also gives us a compelling example, this time from the aviation sector. The industry's approach to mistakes, in short, treating them as valuable data points for future learning rather than sources of shame, has revolutionised flight safety. This mindset shift from blame to learning has created one of the safest forms of travel in human history.

For schools undertaking change, this has massive implications. Creating psychological safety fosters an environment where genuine learning and innovation can occur. When team members feel secure enough to take calculated risks and share their mistakes, the organisation gains important insights that can prevent larger problems.

Our key question therefore becomes: how do we create an environment where people feel safe enough to take risks? Here's a few ideas for a start:

- Establishing clear protocols for sharing and learning from mistakes
- Recognising and celebrating times where mistakes led to valuable insights
- Creating structured opportunities for risk-taking within safe boundaries
- Developing leadership practices that model vulnerability and learning

Understanding how others within and across our team communicate and react to mistakes is central to the Connect stage. Who supports new ideas? What prevents us from taking necessary risks? These questions can help us address the challenges as a school community and facilitate positive cultural shifts.

Building this culture takes time and consistent effort, but it's so worth it. When people feel safe to experiment and learn, they become more engaged in the change process and more committed to its success.

Q3: On a scale of 1–10, how brave are we?

What do you believe is the most important predictor to implement sustainable change?

Brené Brown, in her book *Dare to Lead*,[7] tells us that the level of collective courage in an organisation is the single most important predictor of that organisation's ability to be successful. Successful in terms of its culture, developing new ideas, and implementing change.

In the Connect stage of change, we are building this collective courage. We are strengthening relationships and trust, and courage grows when individuals feel supported by their peers. The more we help others around us feel brave, the more we create an environment where we feel brave ourselves. Bravery comes from psychological safety, trust, and unity. A culture that encourages vulnerability is more likely to take risks, innovate, and embrace change.

These reflections force us to examine our individual feelings of bravery and our collective readiness as a community for tough conversations and difficult truths.

Courage and fear are not mutually exclusive. The foundational skill of courage-building is the willingness and ability to 'rumble' with vulnerability, as Brown describes it. To be brave requires us to know that we have the confidence and support from each other to take risks. The greater the risk, the greater the need for self-assurance. This means creating an environment where everyone feels safe enough to be vulnerable and take those necessary risks.

You will also notice that this question requires you to rate yourself. Providing a number out of 10 to represent our bravery, although seemingly arbitrary, encourages us to scaffold our thinking and consider what those numbers represent. For example, if I feel 6 out of 10 for bravery, what would it take to get to a 7? Or, as John Campbell from GROWTH Coaching International thoughtfully reminded us in a conversation, why did I not choose 5? Positively framing where we've come from and encouraging ourselves to push forward helps us reflect on our progress and set achievable, incremental goals.

Understanding how brave we feel as individuals connects directly to the dynamics of the organisation in this stage. Some might be willing to be brave, but as an organisation, we are only as brave as the one who is most insecure and fearful.

Q4: What's the best disagreement you've ever had?

Change Starts Here

Disagreement doesn't equal disconnection.

Good outcomes are born out of good dialogue, even when that dialogue involves disagreement. The ability to feel safe enough to express opinions, understand differences, and explore their deeper meaning is invaluable. When trust is present, disagreements become opportunities to learn, connect, and develop as a team.

In every organisation, no matter the size, disagreements are inevitable. How we handle them can determine whether they become constructive stepping stones or destructive barriers to future communication. Are we 'stepping on eggshells', limiting our ability to connect fully with our community? How might disagreements actually promote our diverse thinking and the shared exploration of innovative ideas?

Jim Knight, in *The Definitive Guide to Instructional Coaching*,[8] offers a useful framework through his contrast between consonant and dissonant conversations. Consonant conversations, characterised by smooth collaboration, flourish in psychologically safe environments where people feel comfortable expressing disagreements without fear. Dissonant conversations, marked by struggle and tension, often signal a lack of psychological safety.

And constructive disagreements, when managed well, can:

- Lead to innovative solutions
- Enhance mutual understanding
- Strengthen relationships
- Encourage open communication
- Promote diversity of thought

However, poorly managed disagreements erode trust and stifle collaboration. The key lies not in avoiding disagreements, but in developing the skills to navigate them productively. In the Connect stage, this means creating space for these conversations while protecting the foundation of trust we're building.

Understanding Your Team's Approach

Reflecting on how your team handles disagreement opens a window into several key aspects of your organisational culture. When you look closely, you'll start to see patterns in how people respond to difficult emotions and situations, as well as the formal and informal processes that have evolved for managing conflicts. This reflection often brings to light both potential bad habits that need addressing and existing team strengths that could be leveraged more effectively. Importantly, it can also indicate your team's readiness for upcoming change.

Some teams might discover they already have good mechanisms for handling disagreement, while others might identify this as an area for growth. What matters is honest assessment and willingness to develop these skills.

Q5: Where have we done change well before?

We might think we always respond in the moment, but often, how we respond to change is habitual. The success of any change depends on three key elements:

1. Our previous experiences with change
2. The trust we share as a team
3. The systems within which we work

And while we often ruminate on past challenges, our successes can be equally valuable for future change, particularly when we take time to reflect and learn from them together. Looking back at what we've already accomplished builds collective confidence, reminding us that successful change is not just possible, but something we've already achieved.

In the Connect stage, revisiting these past accomplishments strengthens relationships by reminding us of what we've already achieved together. Anchoring change efforts in previous shared accomplishments can highlight unknown strengths that have been gained through working through change in the past and gauge what might need to be considered going forward. Why would this change be different? Is there something we could take with us into this new experience?

With each change, the dynamics will shift; the people, systems, and ideas may be different, but with that comes increased opportunity. New team members, for example, may not be aware of what was previously done and the strengths that were used, yet they can offer a fresh perspective, an 'outsider mindset' on established practices. This enables them to see opportunities for change or notice strengths or areas that existing members may overlook.

When examining our change history, here are some further questions to consider:

- What worked well in past changes?
- Which challenges taught us the most?

Change Starts Here

- How can we blend past experience with new perspectives?
- What change muscles have we already developed?

This connection with our past experiences will create a foundation of understanding that prepares us for any future change.

Notes

1   Crome, S. (2023). *The Power of Teams: How to Create and Lead Thriving School Teams*. John Catt Educational Ltd.
2   Edmondson, A. C. (2018). *The Fearless Organization: Creating Psychological Safety in the Workplace for Learning, Innovation, and Growth*. John Wiley & Sons.
3   Knight, J. (2016). *Better Conversations: Coaching Ourselves and Each Other to Be More Credible, Caring, and Connected*. Corwin Press.
4   Edmondson, A. C. (2018). *The Fearless Organization: Creating Psychological Safety in the Workplace for Learning, Innovation, and Growth*. John Wiley & Sons.
5   Edmondson, A. C. (2018). *The Fearless Organization: Creating Psychological Safety in the Workplace for Learning, Innovation, and Growth*. John Wiley & Sons, p.3
6   Syed, M. (2020). *Black Box Thinking: The Surprising Truth About Success*. Portfolio.
7   Brown, B. (2018). *Dare to Lead: Brave Work. Tough Conversations. Whole Hearts*. Random House.
8   Knight, J. (2022). *The Definitive Guide to Instructional Coaching: Seven Factors for Success*. ASCD.

Jordan's Story

Remember Jordan, the CEO of the Multi-Academy Trust? He believed there was a communication issue in their group that was stopping parents from understanding the great strides the schools were making.

When speaking with parents, students, and staff, Jordan realised that their communication had been sporadic at best. He'd been so heavily consumed with fixing the urgent issues that he had yet to meet with his entire parent body. This was trickier than he initially thought. Parents were no longer as open to meeting as they once were. He arranged a meeting for the parents, but less than 5% attended. While the timing of the meeting might have been a factor, Jordan sensed there was more to it.

Determined to bridge this gap, Jordan opened up various communication channels. He tried to meet teachers and parents where they were, attempting to listen to students by creating student councils, but no one applied. He established parent liaison boards, but only three parents signed up across all the schools. Jordan realised he was in a very difficult position and would have to work diligently on building trust.

When he finally did get to meet with people, Jordan asked, 'When was the last time you felt truly heard?' This question revealed a profound sense of neglect. Many parents and teachers expressed that they had not felt genuinely listened to in years, contributing to a deep-seated distrust in the school's administration. But wider than that, teachers also reported the same when working with leadership.

Jordan also asked, 'What happens when people make mistakes here?' The responses indicated a culture of blame and fear. Mistakes were often met with harsh criticism rather than seen as opportunities for learning and growth. This insight high-lighted the need for a more supportive and understanding envi-ronment. And the community agreed right away that change was needed here. In fact, a group of teachers established a working group straight after this meeting to start to explore the issue and solution.

Finally, Jordan asked, 'On a scale of 1–10, how brave are we as an organisation?' The answers were revealing. Most responses fell on the lower end of the scale, indicating a significant hesi-tancy to embrace change and take risks. This lack of bravery suggested that the school community needed strong leadership to guide them through the uncertainty of transformation.

Through these conversations, Jordan began to understand the depth of the challenge ahead. And it was clear that a period of trust and culture-building was needed before any good change could be communicated. The decision was taken to pause the change for now and work on a culture of organisational safety. To support this, an organisational coach was hired to do six months of intensive work with the schools with a review planned afterwards.

Stage 2: Discover

PERCEIVED
CHALLENGE

1

CONNECT
DISCOVER

DEFINE
ALIGN

COMMUNITY
GOAL

2

DEVELOP
LEARN

DELIVER
SUSTAIN

SUSTAINED
SOLUTION

3

DOI: 10.4324/9781003596141-5

Change Starts Here

Here we go wide. See how the double diamond is in its expanding point here. This is because this is about exploring what our challenge is and could be. This stage is not about decisions; it is about options. What could the issue here be from all of our perspectives, not only that of the sponsor.

Discovery is intrinsically linked to connection. As you build trust within your community, people feel safe to share their thoughts and ideas. And this is why you should be discovering while connecting. Those foundations are key.

During this stage, consider the multiple dimensions that may contribute to your challenge. Seek out different viewpoints and encourage open dialogue. This is a time to uncover feelings and assumptions that may be influencing people's perceptions. You may conduct surveys to understand team dynamics and cultural nuances that may impact the change process. As you gather information, you will also be building partnership principles, like those from Jim Knight,[1] referred to at the start of the Connect section, the principles that guide the relationships in your setting. These will guide your community through the change.

As you go through this stage you will evaluate the benefits and costs of addressing the challenge. Be open to the possibility that you may be missing critical information or that your initial assumptions could be wrong. Actively seek out voices that may not typically be heard, as they may offer valuable insights.

In exploring options for change, we can also learn again from Sam Crome's approach to teamwork in schools. He suggests that teams should have 'shared goals and work products, transforming their sense of collegiality and collaboration, and enhancing their mutual support and accountability'.[2] This collaborative approach to discovery can lead to more robust and diverse ideas, as team members bring their unique perspectives to the table. This can help uncover solutions that might otherwise remain hidden.

As you move through the Discover stage, keep an open mind. Be prepared to let go of your initial ideas and be shaped by what you learn from your community. This is the essence of collaborative change, a willingness to be influenced by the collective wisdom of those around you. The five questions in this section will guide you in exploring the challenge from multiple angles. They will help you gather diverse viewpoints and start to paint a more comprehensive picture of what needs to change and why.

Remember, the Discover stage is about expanding your understanding of the challenge. It's a time to be curious, to ask questions, and to listen deeply.

Q6: What's the real challenge here?

What else?

Picture this. You and your closest friend find an old map for buried treasure in your area. After careful planning, you find the spot and begin to dig. Hours pass with nothing to show for your efforts, when suddenly, the satisfying clink of metal against your spade.

You've found a single gold coin.

What would you do? Would that small discovery deflate your enthusiasm, or would it fuel your determination to dig deeper? Would it confirm your suspicions that there's more to uncover?

Michael Bungay-Stanier, in his book *The Coaching Habit*,[3] suggests asking 'What else?' to uncover deeper insights and better solutions. As humans, we're creatures of habit; this serves us well in many ways, but it can also blind us to different perspectives on familiar situations. In the Discover stage, we need to look beyond surface-level challenges to understand what truly lies beneath.

Our understanding of challenges can become one-dimensional when we're too close to them. Defining the real challenge requires us to step back and explore multiple perspectives. When we have the confidence to dig deeper, to challenge our preconceived ideas, and to truly listen to others' perspectives, what initially appeared as an insurmountable obstacle might reveal itself as something quite different.

This process of strategic exploration, rather than reactive response, helps us clearly define what we're really dealing with, ensuring clear focus.

Q7: What would happen if we did nothing?

This might be the most important question you'll ever ask in a change process. In fact, many changes that organisations pursue aren't actually needed. Asking this question early may save you enormous amounts of time, energy, and resources.

Change always comes with costs and benefits. In the Discover stage, we need to honestly evaluate what would happen if we did nothing at all. This requires understanding genuine need rather than creating false urgency.

John Kotter, a leading authority on leadership and change, reminds us that real urgency comes from understanding genuine consequences. When we truly grasp what's at stake, motivation follows naturally. Yet too often, we rush into change without this clear understanding.

Sometimes change becomes essential for survival. The stakes are particularly high in organisations, where change affects entire communities. The key is moving from whether we should change to how we'll change together. Experience shows us that even difficult changes feel different when everyone understands their necessity.

In their book *Our Iceberg Is Melting*, John Kotter and Holger Rathgeber share a powerful story about a colony of penguins living on what appears to be a stable iceberg.[4] One curious penguin, Fred, notices concerning signs about their home, cracks in the ice, unusual melting patterns, and structural weaknesses that others have overlooked. Despite his evidence, the colony initially dismisses his concerns. They've lived on this iceberg for years, after all. It's their home, it's familiar, and on the surface, everything seems fine.

We won't ruin the ending, but this story perfectly captures how organisations often resist change until the evidence becomes impossible to ignore. Just as the penguin colony initially struggled to accept that their comfortable home was becoming dangerous, schools can cling to familiar practices long after they've stopped serving their purpose. We see

69

this in outdated assessment practices, rigid timetabling, or classroom layouts that no longer match how students learn best. Sometimes it takes a 'Fred', someone willing to question the status quo, to help us see what needs to change before the situation becomes critical.

Edgar Schein, a pioneer in organisational psychology, helps us understand why this happens.[5] He shows how organisational culture shapes everything we do, from classroom layouts to deep-seated beliefs about teaching and learning. These underlying assumptions often resist change most strongly.

Kurt Lewin, whose work revolutionised our understanding of group dynamics, describes how significant change requires 'unfreezing', that moment when we collectively recognise the need to do something different.[6] This unfreezing doesn't come from pressure or mandates. It comes from honest conversations about what's really happening in our schools and classrooms.

Before rushing into any change, take time to explore whether it's really necessary. The strongest foundation for meaningful change is not in the excitement of what's new but in the realisation that staying the same is no longer an option.

Q8: What are we missing?

Change Starts Here

It's impossible to consider every perspective when planning change, but overlooking key viewpoints can derail even our best-laid plans. Group dynamics play a crucial role here: they can either help us explore different viewpoints or work against us.

Werner Ulrich, a Swiss philosopher who pioneered critical systems thinking[7] in the 1980s, developed a framework that's particularly relevant to how we think about change in schools. His Multiple Perspectives Analysis challenged the way organisations made decisions by asking three fundamental questions:

1. What's actually going on?
2. What ought to be going on?
3. What are we missing?

He believed that when planning any change, we needed to consider not only those directly involved, but also those affected by the change and even those who might be excluded from the conversation entirely.

Ulrich's work showed how easy it is to fall into the trap of only considering the perspectives that are immediately visible to us. In a school context, this might mean hearing from vocal department heads while missing the views of teaching assistants, or consulting teachers but not students. His framework pushed leaders to actively seek out voices that might otherwise go unheard, and to question assumptions that might seem obvious to those in positions of power.

Groupthink also poses a particular challenge. When our desire for harmony overrides our willingness to think critically, we risk missing vital information. We might avoid challenging the majority view or make dangerous assumptions simply because everyone seems to agree.

Try to think of change like planting a seed. Those early decisions, about what to plant, where to plant it, and how to nurture it, might seem small at first. But they determine everything that follows. Missing key perspectives at this stage is like planting in poor soil or the wrong climate; problems that become obvious only when it's too late to easily fix them.

This is why we need to deliberately seek out different viewpoints early in any change process. Ask yourself:

1. What assumptions are we making?
2. Whose voice haven't we heard?
3. What information might we be missing?

Even when we feel ready to move forward, taking time to explore these questions can save us from bigger problems later.

Q9: Are we actively seeking other views?

Change affects everyone in our organisation, yet we often rely on the same familiar voices. And the people we hear most aren't necessarily the ones we need to hear most.

Matthew Syed tackled this challenge head-on in *Rebel Ideas*.[8] Through compelling research and real-world examples, he showed how depending on familiar voices can actually harm our organisations. When teams lack diversity of thought, they become echo chambers, everyone nodding along to ideas that feel comfortable but might be desperately wrong.

Syed's work went beyond just making a case for diversity. He demonstrated how diverse teams consistently outperformed homogeneous ones, even when the homogeneous teams had higher individual expertise. Why? Because diverse teams brought different perspectives, experiences, and ways of thinking. They spotted problems that others missed and came up with solutions that might never have occurred to a more uniform group.

Think about your own school. Who do you usually hear from in meetings? Whose perspectives shape your decisions? More importantly, whose voices are missing? It might be teaching assistants who see a different side of classroom life, or support staff who understand the practical challenges of implementing change. Sometimes it's the quieter teachers who spot problems that more vocal colleagues miss.

This goes beyond fairness, though that matters too. Making better decisions requires listening to a range of voices. When we limit ourselves to familiar voices, we limit our understanding of what's really happening in our schools. We might miss crucial insights that could make the difference between success and failure.

Creating space for diverse voices takes deliberate effort. It means actively seeking out different perspectives. It means creating conditions where people feel safe to speak up, even when their view differs from the majority. And sometimes it means being uncomfortable, because the most valuable insights often come from the perspectives that challenge us the most.

Q10: What if we played devil's advocate?

Change Starts Here

Even when we've gathered different perspectives, there's a risk we'll still fall into agreement too quickly. Teams can become echo chambers, everyone nodding along to ideas that feel right but might be fundamentally flawed.

Playing devil's advocate, deliberately challenging our own thinking, requires pressure-testing our ideas before we commit to them. In the Discover stage, this means asking uncomfortable questions. What if we're completely wrong about this? What if there's a better way we haven't considered? What if our assumptions about what's possible are actually holding us back?

Here, we can come back to Matthew Syed's work and his 2019 book *Rebel Ideas* on cognitive diversity. He explores how even diverse teams can fall into groupthink if they don't actively challenge their own thinking. The most successful teams deliberately created space for disagreement and alternative viewpoints.

Think about the last major change your school implemented. Did anyone play devil's advocate? Did anyone ask the difficult questions that might have revealed potential problems? Or did everyone agree too quickly, too easily?

The challenge is that most of us don't like disagreement. School cultures often value harmony and consensus. But sometimes, the most valuable thing a team member can do is disagree, not to be difficult, but to help the team think more deeply about what they're proposing.

To ignite curiosity. To start a conversation.

Because there's always more to discover, more to challenge, and more to improve. That idea can feel exhausting if we see it as criticism of what we're currently doing. But it can be liberating if we see it as an invitation to keep growing, keep learning, and keep making things better for our students and staff.

Notes

1 Knight, J. (2022). *The Definitive Guide to Instructional Coaching: Seven Factors for Success*. ASCD.
2 Crome, S. (2023). *The Power of Teams: How to Create and Lead Thriving School Teams*. John Catt Educational Ltd.
3 Bungay-Stanier, M. (2016). *The Coaching Habit: Say Less, Ask More & Change the Way You Lead Forever*. Box of Crayons Press.
4 Kotter, J. P., & Rathgeber, H. (2006). *Our Iceberg Is Melting: Changing and Succeeding Under Any Conditions*. St Martin's Press.
5 Schein, E. H. (2016). *Organizational Culture and Leadership* (5th ed.). Jossey-Bass.
6 Lewin, K. (1947). Frontiers in group dynamics. *Human Relations*, 1(1), 5–41.
7 Ulrich, W. (1983). *Critical Heuristics of Social Planning: A New Approach to Practical Philosophy*. Haupt.
8 Syed, M. (2019). *Rebel Ideas: The Power of Diverse Thinking*. John Murray Press.

Mei's story

Remember Mei? Mei is feeling frustrated that her history department is disconnected and constantly planning lessons and schemes from scratch.

Mei initially thought this was an issue specific to the history department. However, she arranged a chat with other heads of department and asked for their views. What became clear is that this was a systemic issue: most departments felt exactly the same.

Mei and her team wondered about the impact this might be having on their students. They called a meeting with the parent support group to discuss their feelings about the differences in students' experiences between teachers. Parents reported a general feeling of confusion as they weren't sure what was being taught when and therefore didn't know how to support their children at home.

In a previous student survey, students had reported feeling overwhelmed at testing time as they often weren't fully prepared for the questions that came up.

Mei and her team felt these areas were likely connected. But it wasn't necessarily just about connecting planning. During meetings, the teams also reported a lack of space to collaborate due to timetable clashes. Some team members felt that if timetables were better aligned, this issue would resolve itself.

The senior leadership team realised that this process marked the first time they'd ever met directly with teachers, and one leader pondered whether this lack of direct communication had contributed to the issue.

Stage 3:
Define

DOI: 10.4324/9781003596141-6

Change Starts Here

After we've gone expansive in the Discover stage, it's time to converge. We take all possibilities and ideas generated and refine them into a coherent, shared vision that reflects the collective aspirations and values of the group.

At the heart of this stage lies the 'why' of the challenge. As Simon Sinek says so passionately, 'Why is where we should always start'.[1] Organisations that do are more successful. Why does this matter to us as a community? By digging deep, we can articulate a compelling purpose that will guide us through the change process and inspire everyone to work towards a common end.

Moving from theoretical ideas to a tangible goal can be a challenge; it involves refining our theory of action. Viviane Robinson suggests that leaders have the most significant impact when they prioritise improving teaching and learning, aligning actions with meaningful, outcome-focused goals.[2] This approach not only sharpens our focus but also builds the relational trust and high standards necessary for lasting organisational growth.

And we must continually check assumptions, ensuring our proposed course of action is grounded in reality, so that the steps we take are both realistic and directly aligned with the outcomes we desire.

Refining ideas involves tough choices. We must let go of some concepts in service of the greater vision. Consider the costs: time, energy, potential trade-offs. Keep the community at the forefront to create a goal everyone can see themselves achieving and feel motivated to work towards.

The five questions in this section will guide you in defining a clear, compelling goal. They will help refine your thinking, check assumptions, and ensure alignment. By the end of this stage, you should have a well-articulated goal that sets the stage for the next phase.

Q11: How will this challenge make us better?

Change Starts Here

When we face challenges in schools, our natural response is often to see them as problems to solve or barriers to overcome. But what if we viewed them differently? What if each challenge was actually an opportunity to grow stronger as a team?

Carol Dweck's work on growth mindset transformed how we think about learning and development. In her groundbreaking research from the early 2000s,[3] she showed how our beliefs about challenges fundamentally shape how we respond to them. When we believe challenges help us grow, we approach them differently, with more resilience, creativity, and determination.

Think about physical training. Athletes don't view resistance as a problem; they see it as essential for building strength. The weight they're lifting isn't an obstacle; it's the very thing that makes them stronger. Could we view our school challenges the same way?

Of course, this isn't about naive positivity. Some challenges are genuinely difficult and painful. When budgets are cut, when students are struggling, or when staff are overwhelmed, it can feel impossible to find any silver lining. But even in these situations, how we frame the challenge affects how we respond to it.

Take staff workload, a common challenge in many schools. We could view it purely as a problem to solve. Or we could ask: How might tackling this challenge help us become better at prioritising what really matters? How could it push us to work smarter rather than harder? How might it help us build stronger teams?

This shift in perspective isn't just about feeling better. It changes how we define and approach challenges. Instead of asking 'How do we fix this problem?', we start asking 'How could working through this challenge make us stronger?' This simple reframe can transform how teams approach difficult situations.

In the Define stage of change, this mindset is crucial. This is because we're not just listing problems, we're identifying opportunities for growth. Each challenge becomes a potential springboard into improvement, a chance to build new capabilities or strengthen existing ones.

Q12: If we could wave a magic wand, what would we want to see, hear, and feel?

It's one thing to reframe challenges as opportunities. It's another to actually picture what success might look like. When we're caught up in daily pressures, marking, behaviour, curriculum planning, it can feel impossible to lift our heads and imagine something better.

But this is exactly what we need to do in the Define stage. We need to step back from the immediate demands and ask: If we got this right, what would it look like? What would be different? How would it feel?

This isn't about fantasy or wishful thinking. Elite sports teams use visualisation techniques because they work. Before a big game, players don't just practise physically, they mentally rehearse success. They picture every detail: the movements, the atmosphere, the outcome. This mental rehearsal helps create neural pathways that support actual performance.

We can use the same approach when planning change in schools. Imagine walking into your school six months from now, after your change has succeeded.

What would you see?

How would students be learning differently?

How would staff be working together?

What conversations would you hear in corridors and staffrooms?

The more specific we can be, the better. Rather than vague hopes like 'improved behaviour', picture concrete details: students confidently self-regulating in lessons, peer mentoring at break times, positive conversations between staff and students. Instead of 'better collaboration', envisage teachers enthusiastically sharing resources, joint planning sessions that energise rather than drain, departments learning from each other's successes.

Change Starts Here

This kind of visualisation serves several purposes. It helps us define what we're actually aiming for. It creates a shared picture that teams can work towards. And it helps us spot potential obstacles before we encounter them. Most importantly, it makes success feel possible, not just as an abstract idea, but as something we can actually achieve.

When teams share a clear vision of success, it changes how they work. Decisions become easier because we can ask 'Will this move us closer to our vision?' Day-to-day challenges feel more manageable because we can see beyond them to the goal we're working towards.

Q13: Do our feelings match the facts?

Change Starts Here

When facing challenges in schools, our emotional responses often come first. We may feel overwhelmed by workload, frustrated by behaviour issues, or concerned about student progress. But how well do these feelings align with what's actually happening?

Daniel Kahneman's work from 2011[4] offers a useful insight into this challenge. In his work, he described two systems in our brain: System 1, which reacts quickly based on emotions and instinct, and System 2, which thinks more slowly and analytically. Both matter in schools, but they don't always agree.

Take a moment to think about a past behaviour issue. System 1 might tell us 'things are getting worse' based on a few difficult incidents. But what do the facts say? Have exclusions actually increased? What do the behaviour logs show? Sometimes the data confirms our feelings. Sometimes it challenges them. Either way, we need both perspectives to understand what's really happening.

Stafford Beer tackled this from a different angle in the 1960s.[5] His POSIWID principle (the Purpose Of a System Is What It Does) suggested we should look at real outcomes rather than intended ones. In schools, this means looking beyond what we think should be happening to what's actually occurring.

And we are not dismissing feelings, far from it. Sometimes our emotional responses spot problems before they show up in the data. An experienced teacher might sense a class is struggling before test scores prove it. A head of year might feel community relationships are strained before complaints increase. These intuitions, built from years of experience, matter.

But we need both. We need the immediate insights that feelings provide and the longer-term patterns that data reveals. We need the story behind the numbers and the numbers behind the story.

Try this exercise with your team.

List your key feelings about a challenge, then list the evidence that supports or challenges each feeling.

Where do they match?

Where do they differ?

What might explain any gaps?

This is a sample exercise, to find more exercises, visit workcollaborative.com

This balanced approach helps us define challenges more accurately. Instead of saying 'behaviour is getting worse', we might say 'behaviour incidents have increased 10% this term, particularly during transition times'. Instead of 'staff are overwhelmed', we might identify specific pressure points backed by absence data or survey responses.

Q14: If we could solve only one challenge, what would it be?

When we explore challenges in schools, we often uncover a complex, messy web of interconnected issues. Behaviour links to engagement, which links to curriculum, which links to teaching quality, which links to workload, and suddenly we're trying to solve everything at once.

But what if we had to choose just one? What if we could only tackle a single challenge? This isn't just a theoretical exercise, we are trying to find the root cause that might be driving other issues.

Think about it like this: If you're trying to improve a football team's performance, you might spot twenty different issues. Or perhaps addressing one fundamental challenge, like their fitness levels, would naturally improve several other areas. The same principle applies in schools.

If you are struggling to choose just one challenge, consider:

- Which issue, if resolved, would make other challenges easier to tackle?
- What's stopping us from making progress in multiple areas?
- Where could we create the most positive impact for students and staff?

The conversation about which challenge to prioritise often reveals more than the final choice. Different perspectives emerge. A teacher might see behaviour as the key issue, while a head of department spots a curriculum gap, and support staff identify systems problems. These varying viewpoints help build a richer understanding of how different challenges connect.

But ultimately, we need to choose. This doesn't mean ignoring other challenges; rather, we must identify where we can create the greatest impact. Sometimes solving one fundamental issue creates a positive ripple effect that helps address other challenges naturally.

Change Starts Here

The key here is being specific. Instead of 'improving teaching and learning' (too broad), we might focus on 'developing consistent retrieval practice across Key Stage 3'. Instead of 'better behaviour' (too vague), we might decide to 'reduce lesson disruption during transition times'.

This clarity helps everyone understand exactly what we're trying to achieve and how their role contributes to the solution. Done well, it can turn an overwhelming set of challenges into one clear, achievable goal that the whole school can work towards together.

Q15: What's the cost?

Change Starts Here

There's no such thing as a free lunch.

This old saying carries particular weight when we're planning change in schools. Every change has a cost, and not just the obvious financial ones.

Patrick Lencioni explored this idea powerfully in his 2012 book *The Advantage*.[6] While focusing on business, his insights apply perfectly to schools. Change costs us in multiple ways:

● Time and energy (often our scarcest resources)
● Emotional investment from staff
● Lost opportunities to do other things
● The comfort of familiar routines
● Potential short-term disruption
● Resources and training needs

Understanding these costs helps us be realistic about what we're asking of our school community. When we introduce a new behaviour system, for instance, we're asking staff to step away from familiar routines, manage the uncertainty of transition, and maintain energy through the challenging early stages.

Think about the last major change in your school. What did it really cost? Not only in terms of budget, but in staff energy, time diverted from other priorities, and the emotional labour of adapting to new ways of working. Were these costs worth the benefits? More importantly, were they costs you anticipated?

Sometimes the highest cost comes from not changing at all. Keeping inefficient systems because they're familiar, maintaining practices that drain staff energy, or avoiding difficult decisions, these all have hidden costs that accumulate over time.

In the Define stage, understanding these costs helps us make better decisions. It pushes us to be specific about what we're asking of our community. Instead of vague promises about 'quick wins', we can be honest about what change will require. This transparency builds trust and helps people commit to the journey, even when it's challenging.

Notes

1   Sinek, S. (2009). *Start With Why: How Great Leaders Inspire Everyone to Take Action*. Penguin.
2   Robinson, V. (2018). *Reduce Change to Increase Improvement*. Corwin Press.
3   Dweck, C. (2006). *Mindset: The New Psychology of Success*. Random House.
4   Kahneman, D. (2011). *Thinking, Fast and Slow*. Farrar, Straus and Giroux.
5   Beer, S. (1960). *Cybernetics and Management*. English Universities Press.
6   Lencioni, P. (2012). *The Advantage: Why Organizational Health Trumps Everything Else in Business*. Jossey-Bass.

Taylor's Story

Taylor, an 18-year-old student, was frustrated by the lack of voice that students had in the school's mental health support provision.

During the Connect and Discover phases of Taylor's journey, she and some friends approached the school leadership team to ask for more voice and choice in the mental health provision. They uncovered that most mental health services were previously set up under the umbrella of academic support services. As a result, flags were only being raised or students supported if there was a related issue to their academic studies. Upon full exploration, all parties agreed on the need for mental health to be supported as a personal issue rather than just an academic one.

The first question was pivotal for the whole team working on this change, including teachers, a leader, two parents, and student representatives. They asked, 'How will this challenge make us better?' This was a big moment for the team, where they realised that a focus on the personal, outside of academia, had wide benefits. In addition to being ethically right for students, they also agreed that this was crucial for culture-building within the whole school, fostering a safe, open environment that would benefit everyone.

When envisioning their ideal future, they saw a school that had spaces for open conversation, where someone to talk to about mental health was always within easy reach, where students supported each other, and where teachers could also access mental health support.

How would they know they were successful? They would see and feel the culture shift. Additionally, they would collect data from their existing student and teacher surveys. The goal was clear and set: to create an environment where students and staff feel safe to share experiences and feel supported.

Stage 4: Align

PERCEIVED
CHALLENGE

1

CONNECT
DISCOVER

DEFINE
ALIGN

COMMUNITY
GOAL

2

DEVELOP
LEARN

DELIVER
SUSTAIN

SUSTAINED
SOLUTION

3

DOI: 10.4324/9781003596141-7

Change Starts Here

As we are defining our goal, it is equally important to ensure that the whole community is behind it. This is where the connection foundations built during the Connect stage of the process become crucial. Hopefully, you have been building together until this point, so now is the time to check in. Are there still any sceptics? What do they say?

It's important to acknowledge that you can't always move forward with 100% consensus. However, we can't give you the exact percentage you need. This is something you must answer for yourselves based on your unique context and the nature of the change you are undertaking.

At this stage, you should also think about the journey of implementation ahead. Consider how you will celebrate your wins and what you will do when you get stuck. Alignment will help you move through the change with confidence, clarity, and cohesion. It's a chance to nurture a sense of belonging with your team and the change itself. As Simon Sinek famously advocates in *Start With Why*, ensuring that your 'why' is clear is essential for maintaining motivation and focus.[1]

Alignment within a team is crucial for effective change, and Sam Crome's work once again offers valuable insights on this front.[2] He emphasises the importance of 'crystal clear systems and mental models' for team work. In the context of our change model, this translates to ensuring that all team members have a shared understanding of the goals, processes, and expected outcomes of the change initiative. By investing time in creating this shared vision and aligning team members' expectations, we can reduce friction and increase the likelihood of successful implementation.

Remember, alignment does not mean perfection or total agreement. Instead, it involves creating a shared understanding and commitment to the goal while ensuring that everyone feels heard, valued, and invested in the process.

So take the time to listen, to address concerns, and to build a sense of shared purpose. This alignment will be the foundation which provides stability as you address the problems and opportunities which lie ahead.

Q16: What would Jo say?

You're probably asking, who is Jo?!

Jo represents someone else in your community. We can easily become absorbed in our own way of thinking, missing vital perspectives along the way. Asking 'What would Jo say?' pushes us to step outside our viewpoint and consider how others might see the same situation. This again comes back to Matthew Syed's exploration in *Rebel Ideas*,[3] showing how cognitive diversity leads to better decision-making.

As uncomfortable as it may seem, role-playing in a group setting can make this exercise particularly powerful. When teams take on different perspectives, new ideas often emerge. Whether our assumptions about others' views prove accurate isn't as important as the conversations generated; these discussions build trust, clarity, and empathy across the school community. The process itself often reveals surprising insights about how different members of our school community might experience change.

While we've considered various perspectives through the Connect, Discover, and Define stages, it's in the Align stage where we risk reverting to a top-down approach. This is precisely when we need to ask what Jo might say.

A useful reflection might be: what was my understanding of Jo before this process, and what is it now? Often, we discover our initial assumptions were incomplete or incorrect.

Ultimately, the power of asking 'What would Jo say?' lies in its simplicity. It reminds us that every change affects real people in different ways. It helps us create changes that work better for everyone, not just those whose voices we hear most often.

Q17: Are you feeling sceptical? What would convince you?

▶

Scepticism gets a bad rep.

We often see it as resistance or negativity, but healthy scepticism can be incredibly valuable. When people voice their doubts openly, they're actually helping to strengthen the change process.

'What would convince you?' This follow-up question is crucial. It moves us from simply identifying doubts to finding solutions. It turns sceptics from potential blockers into valuable contributors who can help make the change more robust.

In the Align stage, addressing scepticism is essential. Too often, schools rush past doubts in their eagerness to move forward. But unaddressed concerns don't disappear, they just go underground, emerging later as passive resistance or disengagement.

Think about your own scepticism. Maybe with a change you've experienced recently. What made you uncertain about this change? What evidence or reassurance would have helped you feel more confident? When we ask these questions openly, several things typically happen:

- Hidden concerns come to light
- New perspectives emerge
- Potential problems get identified early
- Solutions become more robust
- Trust deepens across the team

Sometimes the most valuable insights come from those who initially doubt the change. Their questions often reveal blind spots in our planning or highlight issues we hadn't considered. By creating space for these conversations, we strengthen both the change itself and the relationships within our school community.

References to scepticism being 'great when it is aired' remind us that doubt isn't the enemy of change, it's often the key to making change more effective.

Q18: If I wasn't here, would it make a difference?

This might seem like a deep existential question.

And it is, intentionally so.

It pushes us to examine our role in the change process, whether we're a leader, teacher, teaching assistant, or any other member of the school community. Are we truly essential, or are we just going through the motions? Are we contributing enough, or perhaps holding on too tightly to control? Most importantly, is this genuinely community-driven change, or has it slipped into becoming another individual-led initiative?

Some individuals will naturally have a more active role in a change process. Whether it's because of their expertise, their leadership position, or their unique relationship with the work, their contribution might feel central. But does this mean others should feel disconnected, or that the process depends entirely on those few people? Absolutely not. This is where the RACI framework[4] (Responsible, Accountable, Consulted, and Informed) can make all the difference.

The RACI framework, originating in project management methodologies from the 1950s, helps us think carefully about how contributions are shared and whether roles and responsibilities are clear. It invites us to reflect: Who is *Responsible* for carrying out specific tasks? Who is *Accountable* for ensuring the process succeeds? Who needs to be *Consulted* for their expertise or insight? And who must be *Informed* about progress and outcomes to stay engaged and aligned? By defining these roles, we recognise that while some individuals might naturally take on a more active role, everyone remains connected to the change, understands their part in it, and can feel valued as a contributor.

Consider:

- How much does this change depend on me?
- Am I enabling others to contribute, or am I the bottleneck?

Change Starts Here

- Have I been clear about how involved I want to be?
- What would happen if I stepped back? Would others step up?

Here, think about our specific role and contribution within the wider school community. Sometimes we lean too heavily on others. Sometimes we don't lean enough. Sometimes we're not creating the space for colleagues at all levels to step up and take ownership.

Understanding our role, and helping others clarify theirs, matters. It affects how everyone else engages with the change. When one person holds on too tightly, others might step back, assuming the work depends on that individual.

On the flip side, if someone isn't contributing enough, others might feel unsupported or disengaged. The RACI framework gives us a way to avoid these pitfalls by ensuring no one feels sidelined or overburdened.

Ultimately, the answer to 'If I wasn't here, would it make a difference?' should be both yes and no. Yes, because everyone's contribution matters. No, because no change should depend entirely on any one person, whether they're a headteacher or a newly qualified teacher. When you discuss this question with your colleagues, listen carefully to the responses. They often reveal more about your school's approach to collaborative change than any formal evaluation ever could.

Q19: What happens when we get stuck?

Change Starts Here

Not if.

When.

Getting stuck is inevitable in any meaningful change. Unless we're playing it completely safe (in which case, we're not changing anything), we'll hit moments of confusion, overwhelm, or doubt.

This question actually contains two crucial parts:

1. What might we get stuck on?
2. How will we unstick ourselves?

Amy Edmondson's research shows why addressing these questions matters.[5] Her work on psychological safety, particularly in schools, shows clearly that teams perform better when they can openly discuss potential obstacles. When we can say 'I'm stuck' without fear of judgement, we're more likely to find solutions together.

Think about previous changes in your school. Where did people get stuck? Maybe it was during the first challenging week of a new behaviour system. Perhaps it was when initial enthusiasm for a teaching approach faded. Understanding these sticking points helps us prepare better.

Being realistic about future challenges doesn't mean being negative: quite the opposite. When we acknowledge that getting stuck is normal, we remove the shame and isolation that often accompany it. We move from 'I'm failing at this' to 'This is a normal part of the process that we can work through together'.

And this kind of open discussion builds trust. When a teaching assistant can voice their concerns about a new approach, or a subject leader can admit they're struggling with implementation, it creates space for shared problem-solving. The community becomes stronger because we're facing challenges together rather than struggling alone.

There's power in the framing of this question. We are asking 'What happens when we get stuck?' rather than 'What if we get stuck?' This acknowledges that challenges are normal, expected, and manageable. It shifts our focus from fear of failure to preparation for success.

Q20: How will we celebrate?

Milestones matter.

The ability to celebrate progress, both big wins and small steps, plays a big role in building momentum and maintaining motivation. When we plan celebrations thoughtfully, they help make change feel real and achievable. They transform abstract goals into tangible achievements.

Teresa Amabile's research[6] in 2012 revealed what she called the 'progress principle', the powerful impact of marking small wins. Her work showed that seemingly minor progress markers could significantly boost motivation and creativity. We should actively create moments to acknowledge meaningful progress.

A pizza lunch in the staffroom. A thoughtful message home. A tote bag as a thank-you present. These gestures might seem good, but remember that timing matters. When we're drowning in paperwork or overwhelmed with classroom challenges, do these celebrations feel meaningful?

Amy Presnell makes a crucial distinction between 'wellness' and 'wellbeing' in schools.[7] Wellness activities, like chocolates in the staffroom or after-work parties, provide temporary feel-good moments. True wellbeing, however, comes from deeper changes: reducing workload, giving people genuine agency, and creating meaningful progress. This distinction helps us think more carefully about how we celebrate.

Consider these questions when planning celebrations:

- Do our celebrations reflect real progress or just temporary feel-good moments?
- How can we make recognition feel authentic rather than tokenistic?
- Are we celebrating changes that genuinely improve wellbeing?
- How do we ensure everyone's contributions are valued?

Change Starts Here

While intrinsic motivation drives long-term change, thoughtful recognition helps maintain momentum. The best celebrations don't just mark progress, they strengthen relationships and deepen commitment to our shared goals. A shared lunch can be powerful when it marks real achievement and comes with clear recognition of everyone's contributions. But it needs to be part of a broader culture that values genuine wellbeing over quick-fix wellness solutions.

Notes

1 Sinek, S. (2009). *Start With Why: How Great Leaders Inspire Everyone to Take Action*. Penguin.
2 Crome, S. (2023). *The Power of Teams: How to Create and Lead Thriving School Teams*. John Catt Educational Ltd.
3 Syed, M. (2019). *Rebel Ideas: The Power of Diverse Thinking*. John Murray Press.
4 Perfony. (n.d.). *RACI Matrix: History of a Managerial Invention*. Retrieved from www.perfony.com/en/raci-matrix-history-of-a-managerial-invention/
5 Edmondson, A. (2018). *The Fearless Organization: Creating Psychological Safety in the Workplace for Learning, Innovation, and Growth*. Wiley.
6 Amabile, T. (2012). *The Progress Principle: Using Small Wins to Ignite Joy, Engagement, and Creativity at Work*. Harvard Business Review Press.
7 Presnell, A. (2024, September 3). How to develop wellbeing in your school [Audio podcast episode]. In Global Ed Leaders Podcast.

Alex's Story

Back to Alex. Alex's initial challenge was about getting his children to school. His initial solution was to arrange a car-share agreement with other parents at the school.

However, when exploring options, the parent community realised that the school also had some budget for travel and that there were potential bus services or coordination that could be arranged by the school. Therefore, the community decided to define their goal as creating a shared solution to ensure all students could get to school efficiently, cost effectively, and conveniently.

One of the first questions they asked themselves was 'What would Jo say?' In this case, they thought about what the parents of students who lived close to the school would think, would they see this as a waste of money that shouldn't be spent by the school? The community agreed that a conversation needed to be had with families not experiencing the problem being addressed to avoid roadblocks down the line.

They also considered what would happen if the families most affected by the issue left the school. Would this fall down the priority list? This prompted the school to consider how they would ensure the sustainability of the solution. The school agreed to create a parent charter after the agreed solution, which they could add to this solution to help sustain the commitment.

Finally, the community working group reflected on what would happen if they got stuck. This is a complex change with many moving parts. They reflected particularly that things could get heated as there would have to be some give and take, which might make emotions run high when finding solutions. They agreed that the important planning sessions would be facilitated by one of the school's instructional coaches, who could use some of their coaching techniques to moderate conversations and help keep them balanced and solution-focused.

Community Defined Goal

DOI: 10.4324/9781003596141-8

Change Starts Here

We've now gone from an individual perspective on the perceived challenge to coming together and sharing ideas on what we can do as a collective. This journey has taken us from a state of isolation to a point of shared clarity. But before we move on to finding a solution, it's essential to pause and reflect on where we are as a group.

Are we ready to take the next step? What are we feeling as a community? These questions are crucial because they help us assess our readiness to move forward with confidence.

Finding a solution requires the emotional and psychological readiness to pursue it. We need to feel confident within ourselves, with each other, and as a community. This confidence comes from the work we've done to build trust, to listen to each other, and to create a shared sense of purpose. It comes from knowing that we have the support and commitment of the entire community behind us.

So take a moment to check-in with yourselves and with each other. The questions on the following page are a great way to gauge your confidence in the community defined goal. It's important to recognise that your current feelings or experiences may influence your responses, and that's okay. It may feel natural to ignore your immediate response, but in this case, acknowledge or write down the first thing that comes to mind when you ask yourself these questions. If you get stuck, the table on the next page will help you envision this in your day-to-day life, especially when the pressures and expectations are high.

Ask yourself . . .	What this looks like in practice	If the answer is 'not yet'
Do we feel genuine shared ownership of this goal?	When we encounter obstacles, do we wait for leadership permission, or do we feel confident to move forward as a community?	Return to your community conversations. Ensure all voices are truly heard and valued.
Do we trust in our collective ability to solve problems?	When disagreements surface, can we resolve them together, or do we expect others to step in?	Invest time in building trust and collective problem-solving capacity.
Does every member feel valued within our community?	When different perspectives emerge, are they genuinely considered, or quietly dismissed?	Focus on creating conditions where all voices can contribute meaningfully.
Are we prepared for the challenges ahead?	When pressure builds, will we maintain our collective approach, or fragment?	Strengthen your community bonds before moving forward.
Are we ready to take collective responsibility for outcomes?	If decisions impact some groups negatively, will we address and adjust, or continue regardless?	Develop shared accountability and clear feedback mechanisms.
How will we handle tensions and misunderstandings?	When trust is tested, do we have clear ways to rebuild it as a community?	Establish protocols for addressing challenges constructively.

Change Starts Here

Remember: Answering 'not yet' to any of these questions isn't a set-back, it's an insight. Take time to strengthen these foundations before moving forward.

Stage 5:
Develop

DOI: 10.4324/9781003596141-9

Change Starts Here

We've now got our community defined goal, and it's important to remember that it doesn't have to be perfect. In fact, it will never be perfect, as it's an iterative process. Our goal at this stage is to expand our thinking once again and consider what may be possible.

This part of the process is crucial because it allows us to broaden our horizons and think creatively about potential solutions. It's a chance to step back from the constraints of what we think is practical and consider what might be possible if we let our imaginations run free without our natural limitations.

As we explore our options for change, we need to consider the routes we haven't explored, the ideas we might have avoided, and the strengths we already possess in our community. This is a time to challenge our assumptions and push beyond our comfort zones. It's also a moment to reflect on what we might need to stop doing. Sometimes, the key to success lies not in adding more, but in streamlining our efforts and letting go of practices that no longer serve us.

As we expand our thinking, we may realise that we need to bring more people into the process. In fact, if there was ever a time to start bringing in outside voices, this is it. Now we have a clear understanding of the challenge, we are in a much stronger position to talk with external players.

Developing options means creating a clear vision of what success looks like at each stage of the process, defining the milestones we need to hit, determining how we will celebrate progress, and learning from setbacks. Drawing on the collective wisdom and creativity of our community allows us to develop solutions that are innovative, impactful, and sustainable.

As we move through this stage, it's important to keep an open mind and a bold spirit. Be ready to explore unconventional ideas, to take calculated risks, and to learn from both our successes and our failures. We're asking the right questions, exploring the possibilities, and creating a shared vision of success.

Q21: What could we do and what are we avoiding?

What else?

Remember the buried treasure story from question 6? We're returning to it, but with a new purpose. We now know the treasure exists, our community defined goal. The question has shifted from 'Is it real?' to 'How do we reach it?'

Imagine planning that digging expedition again. This time, you're thinking beyond just shovels. Maybe you need different tools. Perhaps there are multiple paths to explore. What if the treasure isn't just in one spot? The possibilities multiply when we start asking these questions.

Earlier, we explored Michael Bungay-Stanier's powerful 'What else?' question when we were defining our goal.[1] Now it takes on new significance as we search for solutions. Just as this question helped us understand our challenge more deeply, it can now help us uncover more creative approaches to solving it.

You might consider:

- What solutions haven't we thought of yet?
- Whose voice haven't we heard?
- What if we approached this differently?
- What possibilities have we dismissed too quickly?

This is where brainstorming becomes crucial. Not the kind where two people dominate while others nod, real brainstorming, where every idea gets space to breathe. Where 'What else?' keeps pushing us beyond comfortable answers.

A particularly powerful question can emerge from this: 'What have we set aside or overlooked that might be valuable?' Sometimes our most promising solutions hide in the ideas we initially dismissed. They might feel uncomfortable or challenging, but often that's precisely why they deserve closer examination.

Change Starts Here

As we enter the second diamond of our journey, developing solutions, there's usually a surge of energy. After all the deep thinking about our goal, we can finally explore how to achieve it. This is where creativity meets purpose, where 'What if?' meets 'Why not?'

And just as a treasure map might reveal multiple routes to the same destination, our path forward likely contains several viable options.

Q22: What do we already have in the pantry?

Change Starts Here

Here's a story you might recognise. In the film *McFarland, USA*,[2] Coach Jim White arrives in a small farming community in California where students spend long hours working in the fields. The school's athletic programme is severely underfunded and overlooked, but White notices something extraordinary: his students' daily lives have given them unparalleled endurance, grit, and resilience.

These strengths, shaped by their work and supported by their families, became the foundation for something remarkable. White told his team, 'You've worked harder than anyone out there, and I promise you, it's going to pay off.' And it did. In 1987, these young men became California's first state cross-country champions.

Families, teachers, and neighbours rallied around the students, discovering a renewed sense of identity, possibility, and pride in what they already had in their pantry.

Just because we're searching for solutions doesn't mean we're starting from scratch. Often, the ingredients for success are already in our kitchen; we just need to find new ways to combine them.

Take stock of what's working:

1. Which current practices align with our goal?
2. Where have we seen success before?
3. What expertise exists within our team?
4. Which resources are already available?

Recognising these strengths does two crucial things: it provides a foundation to build upon, and it boosts confidence by acknowledging existing capabilities. Instead of always looking outward for solutions, we might find that combining current practices in new ways leads to breakthrough moments.

But we also need to ask: What are we missing?

This focuses on being thorough rather than finding fault. Maybe there's a gap in our knowledge, a resource we need, or a perspective we haven't considered. Identifying these gaps early allows us to address them strategically, rather than encountering them mid-implementation.

Try this exercise: If we could only use what we already have, how would we solve this challenge?

This constraint often sparks surprising creativity. When we can't rely on bringing in external solutions, we're forced to look more carefully at existing resources. Sometimes the best solutions emerge not from what we need to add, but from better using what we already have.

Here's some follow up questions:

- How might existing practices be adapted?
- What skills in our team are underutilised?

Before rushing to bring in outside expertise or new resources, take time to explore the wisdom and capability already present in your school community. Often, the most sustainable solutions come from within: they just need space to emerge.

Q23: What is our gut feeling telling us?

While we often prioritise logical analysis, our collective intuition holds valuable wisdom. Daniel Kahneman's work in *Thinking, Fast and Slow*[3] reveals how gut feelings emerge from what he calls System 1 thinking, quick, intuitive judgements built from experience and pattern recognition.

Sometimes, even when all the data aligns and the logic seems sound, something doesn't feel quite right. These gut feelings deserve attention. They often signal underlying concerns or opportunities that our conscious minds haven't yet processed.

Consider what feels right about this direction. What makes you uneasy, even if you can't explain why? Where do your instincts and your logic align or conflict? What patterns from past experiences might be informing your gut reaction?

To understand how these different types of thinking manifest in schools, let's look at Kahneman's systems and how they might present.

Thinking System	Characteristics	School Example
System 1 (Fast)	Quick, intuitive, automatic, emotional, based on experience	A teacher instantly sensing that a new behaviour policy isn't working in their classroom, even before the data shows it. An experienced head of year knowing something is 'off' with a student before any formal concerns are raised.
System 2 (Slow)	Deliberate, analytical, logical, requires effort and attention	Carefully analysing student progress data to identify intervention needs. Planning a curriculum change by systematically reviewing research, consulting stakeholders, and measuring impact.

Change Starts Here

Both systems have their place. System 1 draws on our vast experience, recognising patterns and raising red flags before we can articulate why. System 2 helps us validate these intuitions through careful analysis, protecting us from bias and hasty judgements.

The strongest decisions often emerge when we honour both systems. Start with intuition, what does your gut tell you? Then apply analytical thinking to test and refine these instincts. This balanced approach ensures we don't miss subtle signals while maintaining rigorous examination of our choices.

Sometimes the most valuable insights come from those moments when we pause and ask: 'This all makes sense on paper, but how do we really feel about it?'

Q24: What needs to give?

Change Starts Here

Something always needs to give.

When developing solutions, our natural instinct is often to add. We add new initiatives, new processes, new expectations, and even new people. But what if we flipped this thinking? What if, for every 'yes', we consciously identified what we're saying 'no' to?

This shift in thinking is crucial in the Develop stage. As Arran Hamilton, John Hattie, and Dylan Wiliam argue in their groundbreaking work *Making Room for Impact*,[4] the key to successful implementation often lies not in what we add, but in what we deliberately choose to let go. They propose a pragmatic framework, the Four Rs, that helps teams navigate this process:

- **Reduce:** Where can we scale back rather than eliminate completely?
- **Remove:** What needs to be stopped entirely?
- **Re-engineer:** How might we redesign existing practices to work better?
- **Replace:** What could we substitute with more effective alternatives?

Think of your school like a packed drawer of old mobile phones; we tend to hold onto things 'just in case', even when they no longer serve a purpose. Just as we might struggle to let go of that Nokia 3310, teams often cling to practices or processes that have outlived their usefulness. The challenge is having the courage to let go.

Definition: Bandwidth

Commonly Used Meaning

The term 'bandwidth' has its origins in technology, where it describes the data capacity of a network. In organisational language, it's often used as a metaphor for a person's availability or workload capacity. However, 'bandwidth' can sometimes feel too technical or impersonal, as if people are merely resources with measurable limits.

What We Mean

When we use the term 'bandwidth,' we mean recognising and respecting each person's time, energy, and capacity to contribute. Understanding that individuals have finite resources and ensuring that tasks are allocated in a way that respects their wellbeing and productivity.

Consider these reflective prompts:

- If we implement this new initiative, what existing practice will we scale back?
- Which current activities might we need to stop completely?
- Where could we redesign rather than replace?
- What might we gain by letting go?

When we add without subtracting, we risk overwhelming our teams and diluting our impact. As one primary head teacher recently shared, 'We kept adding wellbeing initiatives until we realised we were actually creating more stress by trying to do everything.'

The Develop stage requires us to be both architects and archaeologists, designing new solutions while carefully examining what lies beneath. This means having honest conversations about what we're willing to let go of to make room for what matters most.

Q25: What would we do if we couldn't fail?

Sometimes our most powerful solutions hide behind our fears. Removing the fear of failure, even momentarily, gives us permission to dream bigger.

If success were guaranteed, what would you try? This simple question can unlock ideas we'd previously dismissed as too ambitious or too risky.

In the Develop stage of our journey, this kind of thinking becomes particularly powerful. We're intentionally shifting our mindset from focusing on solving problems to exploring possibilities. When we temporarily set aside our usual limitations, we often discover:

- Solutions we'd dismissed too quickly
- Approaches we'd been too cautious to consider
- Ideas that seemed 'too ambitious' but might be achievable in stages
- Opportunities hidden behind our hesitations

There's wisdom in understanding our limitations, but there's also power in occasionally setting them aside. As one headteacher noted, 'All beginnings are tough', but visualising success beyond those initial challenges helps us push through the 'birth pains' of new initiatives.

What would excellence truly look like in this area? This single question can guide us toward our boldest vision while helping us identify steps to get there.

Unrestricted thinking doesn't ignore practical constraints; instead, it helps us identify our true aspirations. Once we know what we'd do if we couldn't fail, we can work backwards, breaking down these bold visions into manageable steps.

In the Develop stage, this kind of ambitious thinking is crucial. It keeps us focused on possibilities rather than limitations. It helps maintain momentum when challenges arise. Most importantly, it reminds us that while constraints are real, they shouldn't be the starting point for our thinking.

After all, some of the most important changes in the world started with someone asking: 'What if we could . . .?

Notes

1 Bungay-Stanier, M. (2016). *The Coaching Habit: Say Less, Ask More & Change the Way You Lead Forever*. Box of Crayons Press.

2 Caro, N. (Director). (2015). *McFarland, USA* [Film]. Walt Disney Pictures.

3 Kahneman, D. (2011). *Thinking, Fast and Slow*. Penguin Books.

4 Hamilton, A., Hattie, J., & Wiliam, D. (2023). *Making Room for Impact: A Practical Guide to Strategic Implementation in Schools*. Corwin Press.

Mei's Story

When we last met Mei, she was frustrated by the lack of collaboration in her history team. However, after looking at numerous options, she eventually came to the shared goal of collaboratively creating a whole-school curriculum map. This map would be understood and contributed to by every teacher and leader, giving clarity for their future planning.

As the team sat down together, they began to brainstorm their next steps, asking themselves a series of critical questions.

'What could we do? What else? What else?'

A colleague suggested buying curriculum mapping software. They recalled a past time where someone mentioned using a particular software, but no one had taken responsibility for it. They recognised the need for accountability and a clear leader to drive this initiative.

One member of the team suggested that a leader for the project would help it drive forward. This sparked a discussion about forming a professional learning community (PLC) dedicated to curriculum development. They acknowledged that this would require time, and floated the idea of using a training day exclusively for this purpose.

'What do we already have in the pantry?' was the question they tackled next. They knew they already had a software licence they had used before, but it had never been made compulsory. They also noted they had a training day coming up, though it was currently without an agenda.

When reflecting on gut feelings, the team admitted they felt nervous about the short-term impact of these changes. However, they all agreed that the long-term benefits would be significant. They were willing to sit with a bit of discomfort together, confident that they were on the right path.

Finally, they faced the toughest question: 'What needs to give?'

They realised that much of their frustration stemmed from constantly replanning and repeating parts of the curriculum. By sharing and distributing the planning load more effectively, they could alleviate some of this burden.

The team felt ready to move forward. They had identified a list of potential key actions: selecting a curriculum leader, leveraging existing resources, dedicating time for development, and embracing the collective discomfort for the greater good.

Stage 6:
Learn

DOI: 10.4324/9781003596141-10

Change Starts Here

We've developed our options, and now it's time to figure out what we need to learn in order to turn our vision into reality.

This stage is all about identifying the gaps in our knowledge and understanding. Recognising that, no matter how well we plan, there will always be things we don't know. And that's okay. In fact, it's more than okay, it's an opportunity. We are educators after all. Learning is in our blood.

Learning is an integral part of any change process. It's what allows us to adapt, to grow, and to create solutions that are truly fit for purpose. Without learning, we risk stagnation and irrelevance.

So how do we approach this stage? We start by asking ourselves who knows more than us. This could be individuals within our organisation who have specific expertise, or external experts who can provide fresh perspectives. We shouldn't be afraid to seek out this expertise and learn from it.

We also need to consider how we can find out what we don't yet know. This is difficult and requires us to really reach. This might involve conducting research, running experiments, or simply asking more questions. The key is to be proactive in our learning and not wait for knowledge to come to us.

As we learn, we are likely to realise that we need to develop our team's capacity. This could mean providing training, creating opportunities for cross-departmental collaboration, or bringing in new voices. The goal is to ensure that we have the skills and resources we need to deliver on our success criteria.

But learning isn't just about acquiring new information. It's also about questioning what we think we already know. We need to ask ourselves what we haven't asked, and what might be stopping us from seeing the full picture. This requires a radical vulnerability and willingness to challenge our assumptions.

In this stage, it's likely you will have moments of doubt. We may question whether we're confident enough to deliver the solution, or whether we know enough to move forward. These are healthy questions to ask. They show that we're thinking critically about our readiness. If we're not feeling fully confident, that's a sign that we may need to learn more. But we also need to be realistic about when we've learned enough. There will always be more to know, but at some point, we need to trust in our ability to move forward with what we have. Only you will know that point.

Ultimately, the Learn stage involves developing the knowledge, skills, and confidence needed to achieve our goals. This requires being humble enough to recognise our gaps, and bold enough to fill them.

Q26: On a scale of 1–10, how much do we know?

How can we +1?

This isn't about arriving at a perfect number. Rather, it's a gentle reminder that there's always more to learn. The Learn stage acknowledges that we don't need to know everything immediately; incremental change is often more sustainable. This question encourages us to reflect honestly on our knowledge and gaps, approaching our learning journey with humility.

When we consider our current understanding, it gives us the confidence to take thoughtful next steps. By quantifying our collective knowledge, teams can pinpoint where they stand and, crucially, explain their reasoning. During this stage, this clear-eyed assessment helps us understand the distance between our present position and what we need to know to realise our vision.

Fear often springs from uncertainty. By articulating what we don't yet understand, we transform these unknowns from barriers into opportunities for growth. Acknowledging gaps in our knowledge isn't a sign of weakness; it's a crucial step toward filling them.

Jim Knight's work on scale questions[1] supports this approach of continuous learning over reaching arbitrary numerical targets. His framework helps teams reflect meaningfully on their current capabilities. This becomes particularly valuable as we approach our community-aligned solution, ensuring we stay receptive to new learning and adaptations.

The natural follow-up, 'How can we +1?', directs us toward specific, achievable steps to deepen our understanding. It reinforces that learning is ongoing and that small, deliberate actions build the capacity needed for success.

Q27: Who knows more than us?

When we're immersed in our daily work, it's challenging to maintain objectivity. The Learn stage pushes us to look beyond our immediate environment, preventing the kind of insular thinking that can lead to overconfidence.

This question drives us to identify expertise both within and beyond our immediate circle. It might be internal stakeholders with valuable experience or external specialists who can offer fresh perspectives. By following up with 'Who else?', we keep expanding our search for knowledge and insight.

Pep Guardiola, the renowned football coach, exemplifies this approach to learning. In their book *Leader: Know, Love and Inspire Your People*,[2] Katy Granville-Chapman and Emmie Bidston share how Guardiola consistently seeks knowledge from everyone around him. As Gerard Piqué, his former player at Barcelona, observed, Guardiola learns as readily from groundsmen as from fellow coaches, 'never stopping asking questions, not only of others but of himself'.

Openness to learning from others serves multiple purposes:

- It challenges our existing assumptions
- It introduces innovative approaches
- It reveals blind spots in our thinking
- It strengthens the viability of our solutions

In the Learn stage, this outward-looking approach becomes crucial. It helps us bridge the gap between our current knowledge and what we need to know to turn our ideas into reality. We might run pilot projects, conduct experiments, engage with experts, or explore new research, each approach expanding our understanding.

When we actively seek out what we don't know, we uncover challenges and opportunities we might have missed. Others' wisdom always enriches our own expertise.

Q28: What haven't we asked?

As human beings, we naturally seek information that confirms our existing beliefs. This confirmation bias, while normal, can prevent us from seeing the complete picture. In the Learn stage, we need to actively push against this tendency by identifying the questions we haven't yet asked.

This self-examination helps us:

- Challenge our inherent biases
- Identify overlooked risks
- Consider impacts on all stakeholders
- Examine implementation challenges
- Test assumptions about long-term viability

By being thorough in our questioning, we're more likely to uncover hidden issues before they become problems. This approach helps build a more complete understanding of what we need to learn, rather than simply confirming what we think we already know.

Erin Gruwell's story, famously depicted in the movie *Freedom Writers*,[3] illustrates how asking unexamined questions can unlock hidden solutions. As a young teacher at Woodrow Wilson High School in Long Beach, California, she worked with students labelled as 'unteachable', shaped by gang violence, poverty, and systemic inequities. Instead of accepting these labels, she asked: *What do my students need to feel seen and valued?* This led her to introduce journaling, giving students a way to share their stories and build trust. Her challenge to conventional assumptions revealed potential that others had overlooked. These students, once dismissed by the system, graduated and became published authors in *The Freedom Writers Diary*.[4]

The full picture often eludes us, obscured by our assumptions, biases, and blind spots. Sometimes what we haven't asked reveals more than what we have.

Change Starts Here

Are we missing diverse perspectives? Do we lack crucial data? Have we considered all potential impacts? What opportunities might emerge if we asked the questions we've avoided or overlooked, like Gruwell did?

This process can feel uncomfortable. When we discover gaps in our questioning, it can challenge our confidence in what we thought we knew. But this discomfort signals growth; it shows we're pushing beyond our comfortable assumptions into new territory.

The more willing we are to ask these challenging questions now, the better prepared we'll be for sustainable change later. Often, it's these unasked questions that, once surfaced, create our biggest 'oh yes' moments, those insights that shift our entire understanding.

Q29: Can we deliver? What would make us 10% more confident?

Change Starts Here

Confidence is key to understanding how prepared we are to deliver on our plans. These follow-up questions are vital for gauging the team's current level of belief in the success of the change process and identifying areas that need further bolstering. The first question, 'How confident are we?', forces an honest assessment of the team's readiness and trust in the work done so far. It acts as a reality check on the feasibility of our plans by prompting us to consider whether our ideas are actionable or still need refinement.

Low confidence often signals that something needs attention:

- Greater clarity might be required
- Resources may be insufficient
- Team alignment could need strengthening
- Key questions might remain unanswered

The second question, 'What would make us 10% more confident?' is an actionable prompt. It encourages the team to think in incremental improvements, making the pursuit of greater confidence feel attainable. This helps move us from simply acknowledging uncertainties to actively addressing them, ensuring that the ideas we've developed are not only creative but also realistic and deliverable.

When uncertainty looms, practical steps create clarity. Teams need tangible actions: gathering specific data, running focused pilots, opening clear communication channels, addressing key concerns. Each small success builds trust in the process.

Our plans must balance ambition with reality. The right questions uncover where confidence needs strengthening and what actions will build that confidence. This deliberate approach helps teams move forward with purpose, grounded in both evidence and shared conviction.

Q30: How will we know when we've learned enough?

Change Starts Here

Finding the sweet spot between learning and action is critical. Without clear criteria for when we're ready to move forward, we risk either acting too soon or becoming paralysed by endless research. This tension between continuous learning and the need to act often goes unacknowledged.

Asking whether we can deliver requires both clarity and confidence. Our team needs concrete indicators that signal sufficient knowledge, whether that's completed research, validated assumptions, or expert confirmation. These learning thresholds help prevent us from getting stuck in endless preparation, while ensuring we're truly ready to move forward.

In *The Leader's Guide to Coaching and Mentoring*, John Campbell and Christian van Nieuwerburgh explore creating a culture where learning remains fluid and adaptable.[5] Setting ISMART goals (Inspiring, Specific, Measurable, Achievable, Relevant, and Time-bound) provides clear milestones that guide our learning journey. These goals help us know when we've reached a point where action becomes possible, even as we acknowledge that learning never truly stops.

When we define these benchmarks, we create a framework that balances thorough preparation with forward momentum. The key lies in recognising that while there's always more to learn, we can reach a point of 'enough', where our knowledge supports confident action.

We may even give a final check by asking, 'Is there more?' This serves as both acknowledgment and reminder: while we may have learned enough to proceed, we remain open to new insights that will shape and refine our approach as we move forward.

Notes

1   Knight, J. (2022). *The Definitive Guide to instructional coaching: Seven Factors for Success*. ASCD.

2 Granville-Chapman, K., & Bidston, E. (2020). *Leader: Know, Love and Inspire Your People*. Crown House Publishing.

3 LaGravenese, R. (Director). (2007). *Freedom Writers* [Film]. Paramount Pictures; MTV Films.

4 The Freedom Writers, & Gruwell, E. (1999). *The Freedom Writers Diary: How a Teacher and 150 Teens Used Writing to Change Themselves and the World Around Them*. Broadway Books.

5 Campbell, J., & van Nieuwerburgh, C. (2018). *The Leader's Guide To Coaching in Schools: Creating Conditions for Effective Learning*. Corwin Press.

Taylor's Story

Here's a reminder of Taylor's story. Taylor, an 18-year-old student, initiated a change process for mental health support in school. What started as a mental health and wellbeing support programme revamp evolved into one that supported every member of the community, with a focus on two prioritised groups: students and teachers. While developing solutions, it became clear that there was confusion within the school regarding what to do. Therefore, the learning journey would be essential.

In the Learn stage, the team began by researching successful strategies from other schools, to discover what worked and how it could be adapted.

One of the key findings was the importance of having dedicated mental health practitioners for students. Schools with programmes that focused on student wellbeing showed improvements in the wellbeing of their student body. This insight underscored the need for a similar role within their own school. Not only this, but they wanted to train student representatives who could be mental health first-aiders. The team compared two local charities that offered training and enrolled a group of students on one of the programmes.

Recognising the diverse student population, the team emphasised the necessity of culturally sensitive training. This training would ensure that the mental health support provided was inclusive and respectful of all cultural backgrounds.

Finally, they learned from younger students about the importance of understanding mental health in practical, personal terms. The team realised the necessity of making mental health support accessible and relatable for all age groups, not just focusing on upper school students. Their approach would help prevent the issue from becoming too upper-school-centric and ensure that younger students also felt supported and understood.

Stage 7: Deliver

PERCEIVED CHALLENGE — 1 — CONNECT DISCOVER — DEFINE ALIGN — COMMUNITY GOAL — 2 — DEVELOP LEARN — DELIVER SUSTAIN — 3 — SUSTAINED SOLUTION

DOI: 10.4324/9781003596141-11

Change Starts Here

We're now back in the narrow side of the diamond, where we are refining the developed ideas into a solution that we can deliver. This stage is about understanding what we will be doing and asking ourselves if we have the clarity and confidence to deliver it.

So we've got a long list of options. To start, we need to consider which options feel most appropriate for our community. If we find ourselves stuck in our thoughts, we should ask what would make it easier to decide. Sometimes, stepping back and simplifying the decision-making process can provide the clarity we need. It can also be helpful to consider what we might choose if we had no constraints, our true priorities and most desired outcomes, free from practical limitations. While we may not be able to achieve everything on this idealised list, it can give us a north star to aim towards.

As we get towards our solution, we need to ensure that it plays to our unique values and strengths, both individually and as a community. The solution should build on the foundations we established at the start of the double diamond. We also need to consider what we're saying yes to by choosing this solution. Every choice has consequences and trade-offs. Are we clear about what we're committing to and what we might be giving up in the process?

Accountability is another key factor in the Deliver stage. We need to be clear about who is responsible for what, and how we will handle both the successes and the failures that may come.

Asking ourselves if we can deliver demands a level of introspection and honesty. It requires us to define concrete indicators or benchmarks that signify we are ready to make a decision. Establishing these clear criteria is essential to avoid the pitfalls of both premature action and analysis paralysis.

Deliver is one of the biggest and most complex stages. But if you have followed the six prior stages, you should be in a good place to work it through. The challenge in delivery usually comes when those prior stages have not been addressed: this makes it an uphill battle. So don't skip them.

Q31: Which option screams out to us?

Sometimes, the right solution is the one that resonates with us on a deeper level, even if we can't immediately explain why.

These moments of instinct help us identify the most compelling and appealing solution. In the Deliver stage, we're refining our options, and this question taps into the team's instincts and collective wisdom to prioritise the option that feels most aligned with our values and strengths.

Jim Knight's work in *The Impact Cycle*[1] and *Better Conversations*[2] emphasises focusing on what energises us as a team. As he explains, when people pursue goals that spark their passion and enthusiasm, they're more likely to stay committed and achieve meaningful progress.

At this point, we've explored all possible solutions, but we need to decide which one feels most appropriate for our community and can be delivered together. This approach taps into our energy and motivation for change, helping us identify the options we're most committed to. When a solution feels 'right' without overthinking, it often means it resonates deeply with our organisational goals.

This intuitive resonance matters. When a solution clicks without forced analysis, it signals alignment with our core purpose. The right choice creates natural momentum, becoming part of our daily practice rather than another initiative to maintain. Our community's energy flows toward what matters most, sustaining change through authentic commitment rather than mere compliance.

Q32: If we had unlimited resources, what would we choose?

At this stage, it's tempting to choose the most obvious or comfortable option. But we need to view our choices through both an aspirational and practical lens. While it's valuable to imagine what we could achieve with unlimited resources, the real challenge lies in identifying what we can deliver with what we have.

Imagining a scenario without constraints allows us to identify our ideal solution, revealing our highest priorities and most desired outcomes. By first considering what we would do if anything were possible, we can clarify the essential elements we should strive for. From there, we begin refining these ideas into actionable steps, balancing ambition with practicality.

While we may not have unlimited resources, this exercise helps the team adopt an opportunistic mindset. We ask ourselves: What resources do we already have, and how can we maximise them? We're keeping focus on what we can achieve with the tools and capacity we have.

In the Deliver stage, it's crucial to refine the ideal into something we can confidently execute. By identifying what matters most, we ensure our final solution reflects both our vision and our practical ability to implement it. We are maintaining momentum, aligning our goals with available resources while ensuring we have the clarity to move forward.

The question pushes us to think both creatively and realistically, helping us choose the best possible option we can deliver successfully as a team, finding that sweet spot between ambition and achievability.

Q33: What makes this solution ours?

There is a unique feeling that we have as an organisation. Having ownership over the solution gives it life and ensures it feels authentic to who we are.

This question encourages us to consider the distinct aspects of our chosen solution that align with our culture, and values. In the Deliver stage, it's essential to make sure the solution not only works but truly belongs to us, reflecting what makes our organisation unique. By understanding what sets our solution apart, we can then leverage these elements.

In *Start With Why*,[3] Simon Sinek discusses how starting with 'why' ensures that any solution we implement is deeply rooted in our organisation's core purpose and identity. He emphasises that people are more inspired and motivated by a strong sense of 'why' rather than 'what' or 'how'. This question ensures our plan authentically aligns with our organisation's core mission and values.

When we stay connected to our 'why' throughout the change process, we create ownership that drives both implementation and long-term sustainability. In the Deliver stage, this ownership is crucial, as it makes the solution feel natural and motivating to everyone involved.

Q34: If we're saying yes to this, what are we saying no to?

There's a trade-off here. Every 'yes' comes with a 'no'.

This question highlights the opportunity costs associated with delivering a particular solution. In the Deliver stage, it forces us to confront the reality that committing to one option means sacrificing time, resources, or attention that could be spent elsewhere. Being realistic and considering the energy this solution will expend.

Understanding these trade-offs helps ensure decisions are made with full awareness of their broader impact on our organisation. It enforces a strategic focus by helping us recognise that we can't do everything. It also makes us confront what we are sacrificing as well as what we are committing to.

As we've seen earlier with Bungay Stanier's work in *The Coaching Habit*,[4] effective coaching relies on understanding the value of strategic focus and prioritisation. By asking what we're saying no to, we're forced to recognise the hidden opportunity costs of our decisions, ensuring our focus remains sharp and our resources are used where they matter most.

Q35: Who will tell us if we mess up?

Knowing who will tell us if we mess up and who will cheer us on helps ensure we have both the critical insight and the motivation needed for successful implementation.

This question can be eye-opening for a team. It encourages us to antici-pate the feedback we'll receive, both the praise and the critiques, so we're better prepared to address challenges and keep momentum going. Knowing who will give us honest, constructive feedback allows us to face potential obstacles head-on, helping us refine our approach as we move forward.

Recognising our supporters boosts morale, offering encouragement during implementation and creating a positive environment for pro-gress. When we build teams that feel comfortable giving feedback and celebrating successes, we nurture shared ownership over the solution and its outcomes.

As we explored earlier with Amy Edmondson's work on psycho-logical safety,[5] an environment where people feel safe to speak up, whether offering feedback or encouragement, is key to foster-ing learning and growth. Creating this balance of openness and accountability helps us deliver the change effectively, while also building trust within the team.

Notes

1 Knight, J. (2018). *The Impact Cycle: What Instructional Coaches Should Do to Foster Powerful Improvements in Teaching*. Corwin.
2 Knight, J. (2016). *Better Conversations: Coaching Ourselves and Each Other to Be More Credible, Caring, and Connected*. Corwin.
3 Sinek, S. (2009). *Start With Why: How Great Leaders Inspire Everyone to Take Action*. Penguin.

4 Stanier, M. B. (2016). *The Coaching Habit: Say Less, Ask More & Change the Way You Lead Forever.* Box of Crayons Press.

5 Edmondson, A. C. (2018). *The Fearless Organization: Creating Psychological Safety in the Workplace for Learning, Innovation, and Growth.* John Wiley & Sons.

Jordan's Story

Jordan, the CEO of the school group, saw a communication issue with parents; the schools weren't celebrating their successes as he'd hoped. However, he quickly discovered that the culture was not supportive of change with some issues with organisational safety. To address this, an organisational coach was hired for six months to work with schools on developing a feeling of trust within the schools. Six months passed and each school had been working hard to address some of these issues, so much so that when Jordan called meetings with parents and teachers to kick off the communication change, there was a huge increase in attendance, a sure sign that things were improving.

With this ready to go, the teams worked on the change. Initial meetings revealed that communication was not enough; building trust was essential. By engaging with teachers, students, and parents, Jordan discovered the need for a community-defined approach, involving stakeholders in meaningful ways. With the help of the same organisational coach they'd used before, Jordan developed a plan to build trust through action, giving parents and governors increased access. This strategy aimed to transform passive observers into engaged contributors, fostering a more connected and supportive school community.

In the Deliver stage of this change, Jordan and his team moved forward with a structured implementation plan. They established a parent council from within the parent body, carefully selecting members who were trusted and respected by their peers. This council worked alongside engaged students to create teams dedicated to specific initiatives, ensuring that both parents and students had active roles in the school's development.

To facilitate ongoing dialogue, they introduced a new weekly survey tool. This platform allowed for real-time updates, feedback, and continuous engagement from all stakeholders. The result was a gradual increase in involvement from parents and students, who began to feel more connected and invested in the school's progress.

Conversations in the school were framed around pivotal questions to guide their decision-making. When asked 'Which option screams out to us?', the consensus was clear: empowering parents and students through more formalised leadership roles was the way forward. This solution felt uniquely theirs, as it directly addressed the need for authentic engagement and ownership.

'If we're saying yes to this, what are we saying no to?' helped the team clarify their priorities. They acknowledged that they needed to let go of some of the old, top-down communication practices that had previously alienated the community. They also realised that the school had a lot going on in different ways and each community decided to reduce some of their other initiatives to prioritise this.

Student-led projects and activities were launched, giving students practical, hands-on experiences and a sense of responsibility. Teachers and staff were encouraged to share their insights and suggestions, ensuring their voices were heard and valued.

The progress was monitored closely, with the parent council and student teams regularly reviewing the impact of their efforts.

Stage 8:
Sustain

PERCEIVED
CHALLENGE

1

CONNECT
DISCOVER

DEFINE
ALIGN

2

COMMUNITY
GOAL

DEVELOP
LEARN

DELIVER
SUSTAIN

3

SUSTAINED
SOLUTION

DOI: 10.4324/9781003596141-12

Change Starts Here

As we move into the Sustain stage, our focus shifts from delivering the solution to ensuring its long-term success and viability. This is where we ask ourselves critical questions about the durability and adaptability of our change.

One key aspect of sustainability is embedding the change into our team's daily operations. This means making it a part of our routines, processes, and systems. By integrating the change into the fabric of how we work, we increase the likelihood that it will stick and become self-sustaining over time.

Embedding the change is not a one-time event. It requires ongoing listening and iteration. We need to be attuned to feedback from our team, our stakeholders, and our environment. As we receive this feedback, we must be willing to adapt and refine our approach. Sustainability is not about rigidity, but about flexibility in the face of changing circumstances. Through iteration, we're likely to encounter failures and mistakes along the way. It's crucial that we destigmatise these experiences and see them as opportunities for learning and growth. By creating a culture that embraces experimentation and sees failure as a natural part of the innovation process, we enable our team to take healthy risks and push the boundaries of what's possible.

To further support sustainability, we need to design habits and tactics that reinforce the change over time. We took this idea from the brilliant work at GROWTH Coaching International.[1] (It's the T and H of their coaching model.) This might include regular training sessions, team rituals, or reward systems that incentivise the desired behaviours. By being intentional about the habits we cultivate, we create a support structure for the change.

Ultimately, the real purpose of this change effort is not only for the specific change at hand, but for building our capacity to navigate change in the future. Have we created a culture that is open to embarking on this process again when the need arises?

By focusing on embedding the change, listening and iterating, destigmatising failure, and designing sustainability habits, we're ensuring the success of our current initiative while we're also investing in our ability to adapt and thrive in the face of ongoing change. We're building muscles that will serve us well for now and in all the change efforts to come.

To create truly sustainable change, we need to consider how our efforts are shaping societal values over the long term. As the Common Cause Foundation finds,[2] our lived experiences and the institutions we interact with play a key role in strengthening particular values over time. When designing ways to sustain our changes, we should ask: How can we embed intrinsic values like social justice, creativity, and appreciation for nature into the fabric of our organisations and communities? What habits, rituals, or structures can we put in place to continually reinforce these values?

We must also be aware of the 'policy feedback' effect, where exposure to certain policies and institutions can shape people's perceptions of what is possible and desirable. This creates a virtuous cycle, one driven by intrinsic values, where our change efforts both draw upon and strengthen the values needed for ongoing transformation.

In the Sustain stage, it's important to keep this bigger picture in mind. This is because, here we are not only delivering a solution; we're transforming the way we work, the way we think, and the way we learn.

The work of sustaining change is never done. It requires ongoing effort, attention, and adaptation.

Q36: In two years this change is no longer around. Why?

Sustaining change requires us to think long term, anticipating the challenges that could cause it to fade away. When we imagine a scenario where the change has disappeared, we're forced to confront potential pitfalls and vulnerabilities. In the Sustain stage, this helps us proactively plan for longevity.

By asking why the change might not last, we create space for honest reflection about the weaknesses in our plan. We can identify where the change might struggle to take hold, whether from lack of support, resources, or integration into daily practices. This helps us build resilience into our strategy, ensuring the change isn't just temporary but becomes part of who we are.

Considering these factors early lets us address vulnerabilities before they become problems. We need to stay flexible and adaptive, recognising that sustaining change requires continuous iteration, feedback, and learning.

As we move through the Sustain stage, we must remain open to adjusting our approach, learning from setbacks, and embedding habits that reinforce the change.

Q37: In five years this change is still going. Why?

This question builds naturally from thinking about potential failure. When we picture our change thriving years from now, we start to see what really matters for keeping it alive. In the Sustain stage, we need this long view to build something that lasts.

Imagining success five years ahead forces us to consider what truly sustains change. We need robust foundations, consistent support, honest feedback loops, and deep alignment with our values. It's not enough to just make the change work today; it needs to become part of our organisational DNA, enhancing how we work while being flexible enough to evolve.

The human element is crucial here. When people feel their contributions matter and can speak openly about the change, they become invested in its success. This question therefore helps us create the structures and habits that maintain engagement, turning individual commitment into collective momentum.

By looking this far ahead, we move beyond quick fixes to build something enduring. We're creating the conditions for our change to grow with us, becoming stronger and more meaningful over time.

Q38:
Something new comes along. How do we react?

Change is inevitable. The real challenge is how we respond to it. There will always be something new. As we mentioned in the introduction, change is constant, as is innovation. In the Sustain stage, this question prompts us to consider how we can build adaptability into the very fabric of our organisation, ensuring we stay resilient and responsive to whatever comes next.

Stacy Wallace, an inspiring leader Shane worked with, who maintained a laser focus on results, used the metaphor of driving through a hurricane, a strategy she learned during her time in the corporate world.[3] The road represents our strategy: the strong winds of change will inevitably blow us off course, but success comes from consistently finding our way back to that road. This powerful analogy reminds us that while distractions and new developments will try to push us in different directions, we must stay focused on our chosen path. That means maintaining our strategic direction while being flexible enough to handle whatever the storm brings.

In *Inflection*,[4] Sharath Jeeven uses the example of asteroids and starships to illustrate the dynamics of change. Asteroids represent external pressures; forces heading towards us, often sudden and disruptive, requiring a reactive response. Starships, by contrast, symbolise internal transformations; proactive efforts to lead change, adapt, and shape the future. At inflection points, these two forces often collide, creating moments of tension and opportunity. Success comes when we balance the immediate need to respond with the strategic focus required to drive progress.

The question 'what's next?' prepares teams for future shifts and opportunities. A forward-looking stance keeps our mission clear while creating space for new possibilities. Teams that anticipate change position themselves to thrive rather than simply survive.

Q39: What would failing well look like?

Failure is an inevitable part of any change process. How we handle it determines our ability to grow and improve. Not all changes will succeed, but managing failures constructively holds immense value. In the Sustain stage, this question helps us reframe failure not as defeat, but as an opportunity to learn and adapt.

By asking what failing well would look like, we think about how to minimise harm, extract valuable lessons, and build resilience. This ensures failure isn't seen as the end, but as an essential part of learning and improvement. First, we recognise our natural response to setbacks and focus on making them manageable. Then, we embrace failure as an opportunity for open dialogue, allowing the team to recover quickly and apply the insights gained.

Building a culture where failures are normalised and seen as learning opportunities creates an environment that values everyone's input. People feel comfortable taking risks and experimenting with new ideas, knowing that even when things don't go as planned, the experience has value.

This question helps reframe future failures as steps toward growth rather than setbacks.

Q40: Are we done or just getting started?

▶

The real purpose of this change is to prepare for the next one, and the one after that. Change can set off a domino effect, with each shift achieving immediate goals and simultaneously building the momentum and culture to sustain future transformations. The question highlights the importance of reflecting on our current process and leveraging the insights we've gained.

Key reflections might include:

- If we feel exhausted and ready to finish, why is that?
- How can we shift toward a mindset of ongoing growth?
- What worked well in our approach?
- What would we do differently next time?
- How can we maintain momentum?

Just as each domino relies on the energy of the previous one, our efforts today should spark a culture of continuous improvement, sustaining the energy and vision for change long after this initial effort.

The aim of this question is to encourage us as a team to think about how we apply our new knowledge to future initiatives. It invites us to see the end of this change not as a final destination, but as a stepping stone for what comes next.

An approach that values every team member's experience and perspective creates a sustainable cycle of growth and development where everyone feels involved and appreciated. It reinforces that change is not a one-time project, but an ongoing process, where we are never truly 'done', but always building toward something greater.

Notes

1   Campbell, J., & van Nieuwerburgh, C. (2017). *The Leader's Guide To Coaching in Schools: Creating Conditions for Effective Learning.* Corwin Press.

2 Common Cause Foundation. (2011). *The Common Cause Handbook*. https://commoncausefoundation.org/resources/the-common-cause-handbook/

3 FranklinCovey. (n.d.). *The 4 Disciplines of Execution*®. Retrieved December 1, 2024, from www.franklincovey.com/the-4-disciplines/

4 Jeeven, S. (2023). *Inflection: A Roadmap for Leaders at a Crossroads*. Intrinsic Press.

Alex's Story

Let's close with Alex's story. Remember Alex had a transport issue getting his children to and from school. They had agreed on a goal to create a transport solution with the school to address the needs of all parents who shared the issue.

The school and families ended up agreeing on a co-funded solution with a local bus company and coordinated routes that would ensure efficient pick-ups. It did mean that some parents had to travel a little to the drop-off points, but all agreed this was the best option after reviewing multiple alternatives together.

Now the thoughts turned to the future. Of course, this had to be an adaptable process with new families joining the community. They focused hard on what could go wrong within two years. They agreed that the biggest challenge would be when new parents joined and were not included in the route. They thought this could cause tension, as they had planned only for the families currently at the school. However, this led them to think about how they could put a review cycle in place. They agreed that every 12 months the routes and payments could be reviewed to take into account the changes in families. They thought this would be essential for long-term success. When they reflected on how this programme could still exist in five years' time, the team agreed that it would be well documented in a clear policy, with an oversight committee (consisting of parents and school staff) and a clear calendar of meetings. Having this as a live document, they hoped, would ensure future success.

They finally asked, 'What are we just getting started on?' and agreed that this collaborative framework could be ideal for tackling other issues, such as a new homework system. They agreed to use the template policies and meeting schedules for future home-school collaborations.

The Future

Change starts here.

It begins with you, the person to your left, and the person to your right. It belongs to those you lead and those who lead you. It belongs to those you serve. And it belongs with all of us who dare to believe that we can make a difference from within our own organisations.

Throughout this book, we've journeyed together. That's a collective 'we' that hopefully embraced your whole community. We have explored the complexities of change and found out that, while change is inherently multifaceted, it is also profoundly rewarding when approached thoughtfully and collaboratively.

Alex, Mei, Taylor, and Jordan each faced incredible challenges within their schools. They moved through their changes using the power of questions and engaging openly with others. This led to their change being meaningful and resonant throughout their communities and organisations. Their stories also remind us that we are not alone in facing organisational challenges; many have walked this path before, and many will continue to do so. As a collective, we can learn from one another's experiences and find strength in our shared journeys.

DOI: 10.4324/9781003596141-13

Change Starts Here

At the heart of this book lies a simple yet powerful idea:

Questions unlock possibilities.

Through questions, we open doors to understanding, innovation, and growth. The questions in this book serve as bridges connecting us with the wisdom that already lives within our communities. Trust in that wisdom. Trust that your colleagues, students, parents, and community all hold pieces of the puzzle.

Remember, our model for organisational change is not a rigid framework demanding strict adherence. Think of it instead as thought scaffolding. We hope you dive head first into exploration, adaptation, and personalisation. As you move forward, we'd love you to think about crafting your own questions.

It's there to help you uncover the answers that already exist within your organisation. You have the wisdom, the strength, and the capacity for change; sometimes, all that's needed is a gentle nudge or a different perspective to reveal it. We hope you've felt that nudge and it has found the right balance of push and encouragement.

We believe profoundly in the potential of educators to drive transformative change. Educators are people who change and shape lives. Sadly, many know that teachers can be seen as the least valued professionals when it comes to having agency over their organisations. If that's the case, how about other stakeholders in a school community? As teachers, leaders, support staff, or parents, you are the very ingredients needed for progress, innovation, and positive impact. It's you, not that out-there, elusive solution that others have and you don't.

Remember, change doesn't have to be a grand gesture; it can begin with a simple conversation, a new perspective, or a small adjustment in approach.

Collaboration and community are the bedrock of resonant change. By working together, we amplify our strengths and support one another through obstacles.

And share your doubts. Doing so is good for everyone

We invite you to join the movement of those leading from within. Share your stories, your difficult conversations, and your questions online using the hashtag #changestartshere.

By doing so, you help showcase best practices of vulnerability and the value of every voice. We would love to celebrate those who have become leaders of change from within their own communities, inspiring others to do the same. There's so much possibility when we come together and support one another.

Closing Thoughts

As you lay this book on your shelf, know that this is not an end but a beginning. The conversations you've started, the questions you've considered, and the insights you've gained are stepping stones on your path to leading change from within.

Trust in the potential that lies within your school community. Embrace collaboration, value every voice, and never underestimate the power of a well-placed question. Whether it's a challenging dialogue with a colleague, an innovative idea from a student, or a new perspective from a parent, these interactions are the lifeblood of meaningful change.

We encourage you to continue thinking about how these ideas apply beyond organisational change. How might they enrich your relationships, deepen your connections, and enhance your everyday interactions? This is a great way to model the very change you wish to see.

Change Starts Here

Stay curious, stay open, and keep the conversation going. Share your journey with others, and don't forget to use the hashtag #changestartshere to connect with a growing community of change-makers. Your experiences, insights, and questions can inspire and guide others on their own paths.

We leave you with this:

Change is not an end-point, but a continuous, dynamic process.

It's a path paved with questions, enriched by collaboration, and guided by the collective wisdom of a willing community. And you have already taken the first step.

We want to express our deep gratitude for your commitment to making a difference. The journey of change is seldom easy, but it is filled with possibility, growth, and profound impact. Thank you for your courage, your commitment, and your willingness to lead from within.

About the Authors

Shane Leaning

Shane Leaning, an organisational coach based in Shanghai, works with international schools globally to drive meaningful change. He founded the International School Leadership Academy, co-founded Work Collaborative, and hosts the chart-topping podcast *Education Leaders*. Previously, he served as Regional Head of Teaching Development for Nord Anglia Education's China Bilingual Schools, where he led professional development, quality assurance, and launched initiatives for EAL learners. Shane holds an Executive Master's in International Education from King's College London and is a certified organisational development coach. As a CollectivEd Fellow, Teacher Development Trust Associate, and TEDx speaker, he has extensive experience in the UK and Asia and is a recognised voice in international education leadership. To learn more about his work, visit shaneleaning.com.

Efraim Lerner

Efraim Lerner is an organisational coach and educational innovator driving sustainable change in schools and organisations worldwide. Originally from Australia, he began his career as a community Rabbi before transitioning to teaching and school leadership, gaining experience in SEND and mainstream settings. As co-founder of Work

About the Authors

Collaborative, Efraim partners with schools and organisations to create lasting change. He holds a Master's in Education and is pursuing a Master's in Psychology. An Ambassador for HundrED and member of an EdTech advisory board, Efraim shares insights online, championing inclusive, intentional, and innovative uses of technology for humanity. He lives in England with his wife and children. To learn more, visit linkedin.com/in/efraimlerner.

About Work Collaborative

Work Collaborative is a research and advocacy group focused on fostering inside-out change in education. By empowering schools to lead transformation from within, Work Collaborative brings together a community committed to sustainable development. Their approach values the voices of students, educators, families, and leaders, promoting inclusive change that reflects the unique needs of each school community. Through research, advocacy, and practical support, Work Collaborative seeks to rebuild organisational confidence in schools, pushing back against the trend of heavy reliance on external providers for decision-making.

Change starts with community.
Change starts with advocacy.
Change starts with education.
Change starts with systems.
Ultimately,
Change starts here.

To learn how you can get involved and to download free resources, visit workcollaborative.com.